THE MOONLIGHT MILL
MURDERS
OF STEUBENVILLE, OHIO

THE MOONLIGHT MILL
MURDERS
OF STEUBENVILLE, OHIO

SUSAN M. GUY

THE
History
PRESS

Published by The History Press
Charleston, SC
www.historypress.com

Back Cover: Artist's rendering of the Phantom Killer. *Courtesy of artist Jimmy Bee of Beez Custom Paints.*

First published 2020

Manufactured in the United States

ISBN 9781467146388

Library of Congress Control Number: 2020934439

CONTENTS

Contents

ACKNOWLEDGEMENTS

I would like to thank the Trusty Techs of Shallotte, North Carolina, for their excellent work on designing the website for the Moonlight Mill Murders of Steubenville, Ohio, for getting it up and running and for the technical work with the photographs within this book. Visit their website at www.trustytechs.com.

I would also like to thank my son, David Guy Jr., for his support and assistance with the book.

My thanks also goes to Jimmy Bee, the owner of Beez Custom Paints of Wintersville, Ohio. His awesome artwork has brought life to the story.

I would like to say thank you to the Oak Ridge Inn of Walnut Creek, Ohio, for its beautiful, peaceful surroundings that allowed me to break through the writer's block and let the words flow—it's what this gal needed, so I will be back!

I would also like to say a great big thank you to the *Steubenville Herald Star* for its permission to use various photographs and for its excellent reporting of this story at the time it happened.

1

DEBUT OF A KILLER

JANUARY 30, 1934

Fred Melsheimer donned his blue-and-white pinstriped railroad cap and buttoned up his gray wool coat. He took one last glance around the room to see if he was forgetting anything. An unintelligible mutter escaped his lips as he snatched up the almost-left-behind lunch pail; then, he opened the door and stepped out into the hallway. Sam Hamilton was just coming out of his room a few doors away. The bachelor trainmen had come to Steubenville, Ohio, a few months earlier from Omaha, Nebraska. They worked on the same midnight shift train crew at the Wheeling Steel Plant. Wheeling Steel had a big hiring boom, bringing many workers in from other states. Many immigrants were coming to work at the mill, too.

Sam gave the quiet railroad conductor a toothy grin. He said, "Well, Fred, it's going to be a chilly walk tonight!" Melsheimer grunted as they descended the staircase, spying other steelworkers below and getting ready to walk out the door. The clock in the lobby of the Thompson Annex Hotel began chiming 10:00 p.m. It was still early for the midnight shift to report, but the pair liked to arrive with plenty of time to cajole with the other employees who were coming and going from the mill cafeteria.

The more-than-half-a-mile walk to Steubenville's south end from the Annex at 120 North Fifth Street was going to be a killer, so the men put on their gloves, tucked their faces into the pulled-up collars of their coats and stepped into the inky blackness. The temperature had fallen below zero, and the arctic-like air viciously bit at their faces. They trudged past the lights of Steubenville's busy business district, closer to the infamous Water Street red-light area of town. Beyond that lay the Wheeling Steel Steubenville Plant, with its pungent smokestacks billowing black haze, then barely visible in the midnight sky. Also hidden were the beautiful rolling hills of West Virginia that rose on the other side of the frozen Ohio River.

Fred and Sam tried to hurry their pace without slipping and falling on the thick ice that had formed on the ground. Finally, they arrived at Wheeling Steel's main gate, chilled to the bone after a more than twenty-minute trek. The steel mill yard seemed even colder and darker than usual. Its myriad buildings—lit only by the full moon—loomed forebodingly in the blackness, casting long shadows like ghouls, ready to devour all who came near them.

Fred and Sam, like many of the arriving midnight shifters, made their way to the more inviting interior of the crowded mill cafeteria to catch up on the daily happenings and warm up with some steaming hot coffee. "Catch up with you later, Fred," said Sam Hamilton as he walked through the door and spied some other friends. Paul Elfany noticed Melsheimer as he entered the cafeteria. "Hey, Fred." Elfany waved his hand from the table, where he was sitting. "Come on over and sit down for a minute." Fred got a cup of coffee at the counter and made his way to the table.

"Paul, how ya doing?" greeted the railroader.

"Can you believe they got that Dillinger fellow, finally?" said Paul, in an almost disappointed tone.

"Well, they probably won't keep the guy locked up very long, knowing how slippery he is," Fred halfway joked.

"Yep, you're probably right, Fred," Elfany agreed, nodding his head.

Mill chat usually consisted of the front-page headlines in the *Steubenville Herald Star*. It had been one year to the day that Adolf Hitler had become the chancellor of Germany. The chancellor's anniversary speech was used to tell the world how he was going to rid it of communism and make life better for all humanity as he transferred sovereignty rights of the German states to the federal government by the passage of the "Law on the Reconstruction of the Reich."

In other headline-making news, gangster John Dillinger and his men, having been captured in Arizona, had been extradited to the Lake County Jail in Crown Point, Indiana. Dillinger had murdered a police officer named William O'Malley during a bank holdup in Indiana two weeks earlier. Authorities in Allen County, Ohio, were anxious to get their hands on the Dillinger gang since they had gunned down beloved Allen County sheriff Jess Sarber on October 12, 1933. Posing as Indiana State police officers, members of the gang gained access to Dillinger and broke him out of the

Left: Gangster John Dillinger, FBI mugshot. *Public domain.*

Right: Allen County sheriff Jess Sarber, gunned down by Dillinger gang member Harry Pierpont. *Courtesy of Law Enforcement Officers Memorial.*

jail—but not before they shot Sheriff Sarber. The sheriff's wife had handed over the jail cell keys in a valiant effort to spare her husband's life. Harry Pierpont, a member of Dillinger's gang, shot him anyway.

A photograph showing the smiling faces of Indiana's first female sheriff, Lillian Holley, and Lake County prosecutor Robert Estill with his arm around cop-killer John Dillinger emblazoned the headlines of newspapers across the nation. The slippery Dillinger, with an all-knowing grin on his face, posed with his hand on the prosecutor's shoulder. Bank robbers Bonnie Parker and Clyde Barrow, Charles "Pretty Boy" Floyd and John Dillinger were just a few who had become glorified outlaws. Other states weren't as fortunate as Ohio during the Great Depression, as steel mills kept their citizens employed. These gangsters, who were considered the Robin Hoods of their day, gave a misguided hope to the poor families in the midwestern states, where there were no mills and no good jobs to feed families.

The people of Jefferson County, Ohio, were used to that kind of notoriety, as many local crime stories made nationwide headlines. Steubenville, which was known for its many unsolved murders, was hoping for more peaceable times after Prohibition. The city's prevalence toward violence—Jefferson County's as a whole—was known nationwide, and it earned Steubenville its unwanted moniker of Little Chicago. The repeal of the Volstead Act eight weeks earlier, on December 5, 1933, gave new hope for less violence to the city and its citizens. The national bank-robbing gangster stories were enough to keep the excitement going, as long as they didn't happen at home.

Fred Melsheimer finished his coffee and nodded a so-long to Elfany. He went over to the clock office to punch in; the time was 11:30 p.m. The train engineer made his way alone, passing by the cafeteria, through the mill yard, toward his train. He'd made that walk many times before, often arriving at work early just to climb aboard his beloved engine. It's where he found the most happiness, reliving memories of his boyhood days, when his railroader father took him to work aboard the trains. It was his peaceful place.

A.A. Lashley had left the clock office a few seconds behind Melsheimer and was walking close behind him when he noticed a shadowy figure approach the railroader. He watched, somewhat bewildered, as the figure raised both arms. In the glow of the full moon, Lashley saw the outline of a revolver pointed directly at Melsheimer, who was walking with his head down, the ice and cinders crunching beneath his boots.

Suddenly, there were five sharp cracks. With the sound of each crack, Lashley saw the muzzle flash at the end of the gun barrel. Muffled by the sounds from the steel mill, the gunshots found their mark, as Fred Melsheimer went limp, sinking onto the frozen railroad tracks. Lashley ducked behind a nearby building. The shadowy gunman laughed as he stood over the fallen railroader, jumping up and down. Flapping his arms like a gigantic bird, he maniacally danced over his victim in a ritualistic fashion.

A stunned Lashley stepped out from behind the building and watched as the strange gunman loped off with a gorilla-like gait, toward the plank fence line that separated the Wheeling Steel property from Mingo Boulevard. The phantom-like figure climbed over it and disappeared. Lashley ran into the clock office and yelled at the clock master, "Hey, Mac! Call Bill McCloskey; Fred Melsheimer has been shot." A surprised "Mac" MacGregor obliged by calling the Wheeling Steel police chief immediately, and Lashley rushed back to the injured man.

The full moon shone down on the grisly scene as other millworkers approached. Sam Hamilton was among them. He stared in disbelief at the

Artist rendering of Fred Melsheimer's murder by an unknown killer. *Courtesy of Jimmy Bee.*

prone, crumpled figure on the ground. It couldn't be the same man he'd just walked through the Wheeling Steel gates with less than an hour ago. "Aw no, Fred," he murmured.

"What happened here?" McCloskey inquired of A.A. Lashley, who had stepped up, somewhat shaken, to volunteer what he'd seen. Lashley told the mill chief what had transpired.

Blood had begun to pool around Melsheimer's body as he lay on the ice-covered railroad tracks. His clear, blue eyes were wide open, yet unseeing. A blond lock peeked out from under his railroad cap. His lunch pail still clenched in his hand, Melsheimer was fading fast. Per McCloskey's orders, coworkers lifted the bleeding, bullet-riddled man with care and carried him over to the infirmary. Chief McCloskey notified Steubenville Police, but before they arrived to question him, Fred Melsheimer succumbed to his wounds—the time was 11:35 p.m. The murder of Fred Melsheimer became the first homicide ever to occur on Wheeling Steel Corporation property.

2
ARRIVAL OF THE POLICE

Steubenville officers Captain Frank H. Taylor and patrolman John "Jack" Gilday arrived at the steel mill front gate a few minutes after the call came in. The newly appointed captain, who was known to his men as "Yank," dropped Gilday at the front gate and made his way over to the Mingo Boulevard fence line, where the culprit was last seen. The extremely cold weather conditions had hardened the ground. No footprints were found along Mingo Boulevard. No persons were lingering about, so there were no clues. Captain Taylor returned to the mill infirmary. Officer Gilday was having the same luck; after being led to the infirmary by a mill policeman, he was confronted with the expired body of Fred Melsheimer. His hopes for identifying the shooter were dashed, and Gilday proceeded to take down witness accounts of the shooting.

Sam Hamilton volunteered information about his late friend. According to him, the victim had roomed at the Annex Hotel for two months. Both men had come to Steubenville from Omaha, Nebraska, in July after working together out west. Coworkers all stated that the thirty-eight-year-old Melsheimer was a quiet bachelor who kept to himself. Nobody had a bad or scandalous thing to say about the deceased man.

Gilday went through the deceased man's pockets and found railroad union cards from Chicago, Illinois, and the state of Texas. It was learned from other personal effects that he had served in the World War and was a member of the American Legion.

Left: Steubenville police captain Frank H. Taylor. *From the Fraternal Order of Police, Lodge No. 1 book, unknown photographer, 1938.*

Right: Steubenville patrolman John Gilday. *From the Fraternal Order of Police, Lodge No. 1 book, unknown photographer, 1938.*

"Mr. Lashley," Officer Gilday turned to the still-shaken man, "you say you witnessed the shooting?"

"Yes, I did," said A.A. Lashley as he began to repeat his story. "We had both just left the clock office. I was a few seconds behind Fred. A dark figure came walking toward him. When he got to about twenty-five feet away, he raised both arms, and before I realized what was happening, he fired a gun. I heard the shots and jumped behind a wall." Lashley continued, "Then, the gunman ran over to Fred as his body hit the ground and danced over him. He waved his arms." Lashley reflected for a moment, then stated emphatically, "No, he flapped his arms—like a big bird, did his weird dance, then ran off toward the fence, along Mingo Boulevard. When he ran," Lashley added, "he had a peculiar gait, like a gorilla. His arms were long. It was so dark I couldn't recognize who it was."

"What was he wearing?" Gilday prodded.

"Overalls," Lashley offered. "He was dressed like a millworker."

John Milewsky, who had been behind Lashley, saw the same thing. He echoed the same details that his fellow millworker had, without adding anything new.

Captain Taylor and Officer Gilday instructed all of the witnesses and friends of Melsheimer's to be at the police station early in the morning, after they got off work. The two police officers went back to the station with their findings, which weren't much, to their combined disappointment.

3

THE INVESTIGATION BEGINS

WEDNESDAY, JANUARY 31, 1934

It was going to be a long day; Coroner Charles R. Wells knew that for a fact. Most of his days were long. His wife, Mary, had been very ill for the last couple of months. It was discovered, through a hysterectomy, that she had cancer of the uterus. He knew that she wouldn't last for long. He made sure she was comfortable before going downstairs to drink his morning coffee. His three sons and his daughter, Thelma, were a great help to him. They took turns looking after their mother so that Charles could do his work, which was scrutinized by many. Charles's father, William G. Wells, was also gravely ill with bronchial pneumonia. The old man had just turned eighty years old the week before. The coroner had a lot on his mind, but work sometimes helped to deflect his attention from his personal problems.

Wells's steaming cup of coffee tasted great, but work awaited. It was 7:30 a.m. when Charles left his home. Bracing himself against the cold air, Coroner Wells drove his cold automobile over to the Elliott Funeral Home on Fifth Street to do the task that he'd, unfortunately, performed way too many times before. The number of murders in Steubenville made the coroner's job anything but boring. For just a little while, Wells wouldn't have minded having some down time, but that wasn't going to happen that day; too many important people were waiting to hear what the coroner had to say.

Steubenville police chief Ross H. Cunningham headed to his office a little earlier than usual that morning. Thirty-three years earlier, Cunningham had been born in the very spot that his office, his beloved workplace, occupied. It seemed very fitting—almost like he was born for the job. He had joined the Steubenville Police Department in 1922, the year Steubenville had been coined "Little Chicago" by the national press for leading the nation in Prohibition dry officer murders. Most of those murders were unsolved. After all, people didn't want to turn in their liquor suppliers. Four short years later, in 1926, Cunningham was called upon to take the temporary position of chief of police in order to replace the ousted chief, Blaine Carter, after his alleged dereliction of duty. That temporary position turned into a permanent one, as the devoutly honest Cunningham showed that he could hold his own against the local mobsters. The married family man was going to solve this case—he could feel it.

Steubenville police chief Ross H. Cunningham. *From the Fraternal Order of Police, Lodge No. 1 book, unknown photographer, 1938.*

Hot coffee waited for him at the station; there was a lot of work to do that day. Meeting him at the office were Jefferson County prosecutor Arthur L. Hooper and Steubenville police detectives Thomas J. Dignan and Ernest "Ernie" Schroeder. Dignan and Schroeder, the two paunchy detectives clad in their long overcoats and fedoras, were known as the "Twins" around town. Their reputation for solving crimes and recovering stolen property was well-known throughout the tri-state area. They were as confident as the chief was that the mill murder would be solved.

The group of lawmen began interviewing the witnesses and acquaintances of Fred Melsheimer, which lasted well into the evening. Motives were tossed around by the detectives, but a lover's triangle and Melsheimer being put "on the spot" by a hired assassin topped the list, though

Jefferson county coroner Charles R. Wells. *Courtesy of the Steubenville Herald Star, 1934.*

acquaintances of Melsheimer said he was a quiet bachelor. Nothing new was gained from another day-long interrogation of the witnesses.

Coroner Wells arrived at police headquarters in the early afternoon to hold a formal inquest. Reporters had gathered from area newspapers, and they were eagerly awaiting the results of that inquest. Cornoner Wells said:

> *The autopsy that I performed on the Wheeling Steel shooting victim, Fred Melsheimer, at the Elliott Funeral Home this morning resulted in these findings. He was struck by three of the reported five bullets fired from a .38-caliber revolver. He was struck once in the left arm, near his shoulder, once in the right side, and one bullet pierced his heart, clipping off a piece of his liver. That is the shot that killed him. Two of the shells were recovered and sent to ballistics expert David Cowles in Cleveland for ballistics testing. The firearm was not recovered, suggesting the perpetrator still has it in his possession. The death of Fred Melsheimer has been ruled a homicide.*

After thanking the coroner and dismissing the reporters, Ross Cunningham addressed his group of investigators. "Now, let's go over to the mill and look at the scene. Maybe somebody missed something." The elite of Jefferson County's lawmen exited the chief's office and accompanied him on the short trip to the mill in his automobile. Upon their arrival, the men walked through the gate and were met by mill police chief Bill McCloskey. He took them to the cafeteria, where they began retracing Melsheimer's steps. McCloskey offered his and his men's service to the police. "My men and I will be happy to assist you in any way we can, Chief Cunningham," McCloskey offered as he handed over some etchings of footprints that he had drawn the night before. He explained, "Sir, these are tracings of the footprints around the body. You can see how they're going in different directions, just like Lashley had described of the gunman dancing, wildly, over the body." He finished by saying, "I thought you might be able to use them." Cunningham took the etchings and thanked McCloskey for his observation. It was one that had been overlooked by his own men, but in their defense, by the time Steubenville police had arrived, many millworkers had walked all over that area.

"He was attacked here," Tom Dignan pointed to the ground, where the pool of blood was still evident. It was a frozen, eerie reminder of the gruesome event from the night before. The spot where the perpetrator had fled to his escape was between the cafeteria and the mill office, about two hundred feet from the plank fenceline. Satisfied with the visuals of the crime scene, the investigators made their way back to the municipal building.

The next day, two days after the murder, the lawmen met again in the chief's office. This time, John Melsheimer, the brother of the victim, joined them. The Chicago stockbroker had arrived in town by train to take his younger brother back home for burial. Extensive questioning by the team of investigators brought nothing new to light. They learned that Melsheimer had travelled to numerous places out west, including Iowa, Nebraska, Minnesota and Texas. The guy was a war hero and had been a sergeant and machine gunner with the 318th Machine Gun Infantry during the World War. He had survived many horrendous battles during the war. He had no enemies, no steamy love triangles and no criminal activity in his past. He was just a great guy who kept to himself and loved the railroad. John Melsheimer, the sole survivor of the Melsheimer family, left for Chicago the next morning, accompanying his baby brother on his last train ride. Fred Stephen Melsheimer's final stop was Evergreen Cemetery.

On February 7, Prosecutor Hooper and Coroner Wells urged the Jefferson County commissioners to post a $500 reward for information leading to the capture and conviction of the mill shooter. They stated that, in the past year, six murders had taken place in the county. Only one, the murder of Yorkville mayor Benjamin Oliver, had received an indictment. The commissioners agreed to post the reward, hoping it would bring in useful information from other sources. The investigators eventually chalked the murder up to a love triangle. They hoped that's all it was—a one-time crime. Maybe the killer had left town. Maybe it was over—just maybe.

4

LIFE GOES ON

While police continued to work the mill murder case and all the other cases that had been backing up, February took its toll on Jefferson County's coroner. Charles Wells's wife, Mary Jane, had taken a turn for the worse, and on Friday, February 9, she passed away at their home at 1170 Sycamore Street. She was just forty-six years old. Mary Jane was buried on February 12, at Union Cemetery. That same day, William Wells, Charles's father, died, and his funeral was held three days later. While the coroner had to keep working, his children were his strength and he was theirs. They had their own lives now—he would be okay. He made sure they knew that.

Meanwhile, millworkers went to work, looking over their shoulders all the while. Many wondered if there were going to be more shootings. They weren't as confident and hopeful as the cops were that it was a one-time thing. But life went on. People had to pay their bills.

Detective Thomas Dignan and his partner, Ernest Schroeder, acting on a tip, searched the room of a man whose name had been given to them by a millworker. They found nothing incriminating. The millworker, Harold Morken, insisted that he found the man responsible for Fred Melsheimer's murder. After taking the man, David Dasco, to the city jail for questioning and finding nothing in his room, he was released. Over the past few months, Dignan and Schroeder had tirelessly questioned thirty railroaders who were coworkers and friends of Melsheimer's. They gained very little helpful information. February passed without any strange incidents, and March was almost over. Life was getting back to normal. The stress level of Wheeling Steel millworkers was returning to a manageable state.

5

A KILLER RETURNS

MARCH 25, 1934

Midnight shift workers began gathering around 10:30 p.m. in the Wheeling Steel cafeteria. The weather was getting warmer, and tensions were lessening with each passing day. The mill chatter was getting back to normal with the excitement over national and world events. Some still talked about the mill shooter, wondering if he could be sitting among them. The *Herald Star* newspapers, over the past few days, had been centered on gangster John Dillinger, who was still on the run from his latest escape from the Lake County Jail in Crown Point, Indiana. The lady sheriff, Lynn Holley, was left to suffer the humiliating consequences of the infamous photograph of her and Prosecutor Estill playing pals with the cunning gangster. Meanwhile, three members of Dillinger's gang were tried in Lima, Ohio, for the murder of Allen County sheriff Jess Saber. Millworkers marveled at the fact that there didn't seem to be a jail that could hold Dillinger. While authorities in Indiana, Ohio, Illinois and the surrounding states were following leads on numerous Dillinger sightings, two members of his gang, Harry Pierpont and Charles Makley, received the death penalty, while a third man, Russell Clark, received life in prison.

At that time, Adolf Hitler had just pulled Germany out of the League of Nations, and tensions in Austria, between Chancellor Englebert Dolfuss and Prince Ernest von Starhemberg, were high. Dolfuss had shut down the Nazi Party in Austria in 1933. The socialist uprising that occurred as the prince and Hitler prepared to join forces that February brought a lot of bloodshed to Austrians. Hitler had begun his spread of Nazism. Italy was next in Hitler's sights.

The tall, lanky bachelor James Barnett was a Wheeling Steel railroad employee, and he walked leisurely to the mill from his rooming house at 128 North High Street, as he'd done for the last six months. The amiable man arrived at the mill gates, waving at the mill police stationed there. He noted how the mill force had doubled since the death of Fred Melsheimer. He clocked in at 11:30 p.m. and walked into the cafeteria for some coffee; he listened as some of the guys talked about the sentencing of Harry Pierpont and Charles Makley, who were to die in Ohio's electric chair. A few minutes later, Barnett bid the others a good night and strolled on to his job site. It was a clear night, with a beautiful full moon. Flames leapt from the blast furnace and were a sharp contrast to the darkness. Like his coworker Fred Melsheimer, Barnett loved the trains and his job. He periodically changed the routes he took through the mill, just to break up his routine. Maybe that was something instilled in him by his military training. Not unlike Melsheimer, Barnett was also a World War veteran.

The time was 11:38 p.m. Barnett had reached his destination and climbed the long set of stone steps to the changing shack, behind the blast furnace. Barnett was on the ninth step from the top when a dark figure came out of the shadows from behind a stack of wooden crates. The figure was mumbling gibberish as he raised his arms and fired. Barnett fell hard onto the stone staircase as a bullet entered his right hip. The gunman climbed up to him. Standing over the wounded man, he fired again; the bullet struck Barnett in the abdomen. Barnett's attacker kicked him several times in the face. Satisfied that his ambushed prey was dead, the shadowy phantom flapped his arms wildly as he danced his ritualistic jig. Muttering and laughing, he loped away with an ape-like gait, toward the Ohio River, as the glowing light of the full moon streamed across the dark mill yards.

Millworkers in the immediate area heard the gunshots that had been muffled by sounds from the blast furnace. Those closest to James Barnett heard him yelling for help. By some miracle, the twice-shot Barnett was still alive and conscious. Some carried the wounded Barnett to the infirmary, and others ran after the gunman. Still others ran to get the mill police. The millworkers' fear of the gunman returning had just become a reality. He was back, and it was clear that he wasn't going away. He had to be stopped.

McCloskey was notified of the second incident and alerted Steubenville police right away. He ran to the infirmary, where Barnett had been taken. He began questioning the wounded man. "Did you get a look at the guy?" Barnett, who was still conscious after getting shot twice and beaten in the face, gave a sketchy description. "He was tall and wore a slicker and cap, you know, like you mill police wear. I didn't get a good look at his face, though." Barnett had been shot in the hip and the abdomen. He was paralyzed from the shot to the hip, which had travelled down his leg.

The morning after the second mill shooting, James Barnett was visited by Chief Cunningham, Sheriff Ray B. Long and Jefferson County prosecutor Arthur Hooper. Barnett was under heavy guard at Ohio Valley Hospital. Police feared that once the shooter learned that his second victim was alive, he would come back to finish the job. "Are you sure you don't know something about your buddy's murder?" Sheriff Long queried. "You know, he may want to shut you up for something you know."

"No sir, nothing," was Barnett's reply. "I knew Melsheimer in passing, but we weren't really friends or anything." Barnett paused for a moment, then continued, "The guy shot me, then ran up the tracks. Not away from the mill but running toward it. My guess is that he works in the mill. I wouldn't be surprised if he came back in and was one of the guys who carried me out on the stretcher. That guy's shrewd. He probably lingers outside the cafeteria then follows whoever comes out."

"You may very well be right," Cunningham replied. "Good observation on your part, considering what you'd just been through."

Prosecutor Hooper looked at James Barnett and said, "Yes, sir, Barnett, you're a lucky man. That first shot should have killed you. It shattered the crystal on your watch fob before travelling down your leg. If you'd been wearing another kind of watch, you might not have been so lucky."

James Barnett, the second victim and survivor of the Phantom Killer. *Courtesy of the* Steubenville Herald Star, *1934.*

Left: Steubenville patrolman David Lyle guarded James Barnett. *From the Fraternal Order of Police, Lodge No. 1 book, unknown photographer, 1938.*

Right: Steubenville patrolman Sam Baker guarded James Barnett. *From the Fraternal Order of Police, Lodge No. 1 book, unknown photographer, 1938.*

"Lucky! You call this lucky?" Barnett chuckled, with the ever-present twinkle still in his eye. Though the man was remarkably resilient, and still maintained his big, toothy grin, all the lawmen knew he was feeling the pain of never walking or working again. His days on the trains were over. The gunman had paralyzed him from the waist down. Hooper looked down, somewhat sheepishly. He regretted making that statement, but it was too late to take it back. Barnett handled it well.

Before they left, the lawmen did tell Barnett that a mill policeman's uniform had been stolen the day before. That fact, alone, was chilling. The killer then had the freedom of movement throughout the mill without being contested.

Chief Cunningham advised Barnett that Steubenville police officers Sam Baker and David Lyle were going to be taking turns, standing guard over him, while he was in the hospital. "Oh," Cunningham added, "the press will probably be here soon, just so you know."

6

THE NEW SHERIFF

T
he newly elected sheriff of thirty days had his work cut out for him. Jefferson County's notorious reputation for crime and corruption was not lost on the thirty-three-year-old Ray Bliss Long. He'd served as a deputy under Sheriff William "Billy" Yost from 1931 to 1933, during Prohibition. Just before the repeal of the Prohibition Act (or the Volstead Act), a month prior to his swearing in, Long helped investigate the murder of Yorkville mayor Benjamin Oliver. Frank Romano, who the sheriff figured was the mayor's killer, had gone to trial, but after a forty-six-minute deliberation, he was acquitted by a jury and set free on March 9, 1934. Romano's co-conspirator, Thomas Viola, was released from jail after that verdict, and he was not tried. That was a bitter pill to swallow, but Sheriff Long knew from past experiences that that's how things went in Jefferson County. It was tough to beat the mob, but these two mill incidents didn't seem like mob hits.

Ray B. Long was also a World War veteran. He had served in the army and witnessed the battle at Meuse-Argonne in France. This military connection gave him a special tie to the two victims, a tie that made him determined to solve the case. Sheriff Long, like the police chief, was a married family man who was devoutly honest and dedicated to his job.

Jefferson County sheriff Ray Bliss Long, 1930. *From the collection of Susan Guy, unknown photographer.*

7

AFTERMATH OF THE SECOND SHOOTING

On Monday afternoon, the day after forty-two-year-old bachelor James Barnett was shot, *Steubenville Herald Star* reporters were allowed into his room for the scoop on the story. Barnett was still alert, though the Steubenville lawmen had already questioned him earlier that morning.

"Do you know who shot you?" was the first question fired at Barnett.

"No, I don't," was the victim's reply.

"Does anyone have a grudge against you that might want to see you dead?" another reporter asked.

"No," was his short reply.

Barnett asked the reporters if a certain man, who was unnamed in the newspapers, had been arrested by police yet. "I'm not accusing this man," Barnett said, "but he may hold the key to this whole thing." It was clarified that the police were looking for this unidentified man.

Sam Hamilton, a friend of both victims and a member of the same train crew, refused to go back to work on the Monday night after the shooting. Fearful that he could be the third victim of the mysterious mill shooter, Hamilton told reporters that he was leaving Steubenville.

Wheeling Steel Corporation urged Chief McCloskey and his men to double their vigilance and commended the Jefferson County prosecutor for his fine work. Since the Melsheimer shooting, the prosecutor had interviewed seventy-five men from the mill. Everyone was coming together to find a quick solution to these tragic incidents, which were having a bad effect on the midnight shift's morale.

Left: Steubenville police detective Thomas J. Dignan, 1938. *From the Fraternal Order of Police, Lodge No. 1 book, unknown photographer.*

Right: Steubenville police detective Ernest Schroeder, 1938. *From the Fraternal Order of Police, Lodge No. 1 book, unknown photographer.*

On April 2, Steubenville mayor James C. McMaster held a "crime conference" at city hall. The conference was open to all law enforcement personnel who were involved with the investigation into the mill shootings. This was a chance to get all the information known about the Melsheimer and Barnett cases out on the table and throw around ideas of who may be behind the shootings. Chief Cunningham informed those in attendance that two men had been taken into custody at the YMCA and had been held in the city jail until they could be checked out. The men, James Hartman of Pontiac, Michigan, and Frank Williams, whose address was unknown, had roomed there. James Barnett had also formerly roomed at the YMCA. Police were looking into a possible connection between the men. The chief clarified that they were not considered suspects.

In attendance at the mayor's crime conference were representatives of Wheeling Steel Corporation, including Clifford Smith, the yardmaster, and J.H. King, the chief of Wheeling Steel police. Representing the county were Prosecutor Arthur Hooper and Sheriff Ray B. Long. The city officials present were Mayor McMaster, Safety Director James Madigan and Service

Director William Hamilton. Police Chief Cunningham brought with him the following members of the police department: Lieutenant Marshall Jack, Sergeant William Consol, Detectives Thomas Dignan and Ernest Schroeder and Patrolmen Robert Doyle, William Dunn and John Gilday.

One new item of evidence came out at the conference; a bullet had been found that was fired at James Barnett. Prosecutor Hooper was having it sent to David Cowles, the Cleveland ballistics expert who had examined the bullets from the Melsheimer case. The Barnett bullet would be compared to it to determine if it came from the same gun.

Eleven special officers were sworn in by Mayor McMaster on April 23, and they were bonded to carry firearms. They were hired to work the patrol at the Steubenville Steel Plant, also known as the LaBelle Plant, as a direct result of the conference.

On April 28, Robert McCoy was arrested at the City Rescue Mission after telling people there that Melsheimer and Barnett were shot because they were secret service agents and after representing himself as a federal agent. After taking him into custody, police found out that he was wanted on a check forgery charge. After being contacted by police, the accuser declined to press charges. Satisfied that McCoy had nothing to do with the shootings, he was later released.

With all suspects released and no new information, law enforcement officials admitted they were at a standstill.

8

THIRD TIME'S A CHARM

JULY 1, 1934

A pril, May and June went by at Wheeling Steel's Steubenville plant without any sign of the mysterious gunman. But that didn't mean that he wasn't on the minds of every millworker there. Some men had quit the mill; some of them had even moved away. Others had to stick it out and hope they weren't the next victim. They had families to feed. They knew they were lucky to have a job—this was during the Great Depression. Others were not so lucky to have these kinds of jobs. Men resorted to arming themselves with weapons. They walked in pairs or trios—anything to stay safe and thwart an attack. Except for carrying weapons, these were safety precautions preached by Wheeling Steel management.

On Sunday, July 1, the full moon shone down on Steubenville. Ray and Dorothy Kochendarfer pulled up to their house at 531 Union Avenue after a fun evening out. It was 10:45 p.m. They hurried into the house, and Dorothy packed his lunch as Ray got his work clothes together. He worked the midnight shift in the open-hearth department. The couple kissed goodnight, and Dorothy stood at the door, watching him leave. "Night, Dottie. Love ya," Ray smiled, with a twinkle in his eye, as he climbed into his automobile.

The millworker headed downtown, toward the mill from his Pleasant Heights neighborhood. He stopped to pick up John Millsop, who was waiting at the corner of Fourth and Adams Streets. They arrived at Wheeling Steel a few minutes later, along with the usual throng of midnight shifters, and they parted ways at the mill gate. Kochendarfer went to the cafeteria, while Millsop went straight to the clock office.

While in the cafeteria, Kochendarfer met up with his coworker William "Wild Bill" Messer, who had driven to work with James Porter. He and Porter had also parted ways at the mill gate. Kochendarfer and Messer drank coffee and relaxed for a few minutes, mingling with incoming and outgoing workers. Mill chat was grim, as the newspaper headlines relayed that hundreds of executions were taking place in Germany. Hitler was a dangerous man. His Nazi policies were catching on with other power-hungry dictators, and other European leaders only dared to defy him.

The more popular topic was Dillinger. The slippery criminal was still eluding cops all over the Midwest. Debonair John Dillinger seemed to fascinate everybody. His personality allowed him to charm his way in and out of trouble. Millworkers chuckled as they marveled at his craftiness. Kochendarfer and Messer, like many other men who were sitting in the cafeteria, sipping their coffee, just listened. They listened as men talked of the gangster's infamous escapades in an almost idolizing manner.

Half an hour later, the two men made their way toward the open-hearth department, where they both had worked for some time. About fifty feet from their destination, a dark figure stepped out from behind a stack of barrels and began firing at them. Both men slumped to the ground. The sniper unloaded all five bullets into the pair before spinning around and leveling the weapon at a startled James Stewart. Stewart had been washing up, preparing to go home, when he heard what he thought were firecrackers exploding. It was only three days until the Fourth of July, so he stepped outside the electrical shop to see them. He hadn't expected to be confronting a murderer, but as he did so, the gunman pulled the trigger. Wide-eyed, Stewart stared down the barrel of the still-smoking revolver, aware that it was probably the last sight he would ever see. However, the weapon misfired, and Stewart was frozen.

Unfazed, the gunman turned and dashed toward the Ohio River. A few steelworkers who heard the shots and saw what happened sent up an alarm to the guard on the bridge. As was arranged during the mayor's crime conference, whistles around the mill began blowing. Paul Cash and Gilbert Porreca, both open-hearth employees, gave chase, trying to capture the fleeing man, but they were unable to catch him. For the third time, he had successfully eluded capture and identification. Most of the workers in the area couldn't hear the gunfire over noises of the mill, but they saw the chase. They knew that the ghost gunner had struck again.

The pursuers of the gunman returned to the disturbing sight of their fallen coworkers bathed in blood under the glow of another full moon. Carefully,

Ray Kochendarfer (*above, left*) and William "Wild Bill" Messer (*above, right*), the third and fourth victims of the Phantom. *Courtesy of the* Steubenville Herald Star, *1934.*

Right: James Stewart, a witness to the Kochendarfer-Messer murders. He almost became the fifth victim of the Phantom Killer. *Courtesy of the* Steubenville Herald Star, *1934.*

the latest victims of the elusive mill shooter were carried to the infirmary. It was evident that "Wild Bill" Messer was already dead. Ray Kochendarfer was clinging to life as they arrived at the infirmary, but he succumbed to his injuries shortly after his arrival. The time of the attack was 11:35 p.m.

9

INTERROGATIONS BEGIN AGAIN

In a scenario that had become all too familiar, millworkers were saddened, frightened, outraged and ready to quit as police officers began pouring into the mill. In addition to mill police, Captain Frank Taylor, Sergeant William Consol and Patrolman Sam Baker from the Steubenville Police Department were the first on the scene. They were quickly followed by Chief Cunningham, Sheriff Long, Prosecutor Hooper, Coroner Wells, Detectives Dignan and Schroeder and Jefferson County deputy Joseph Morrow. Wheeling Steel Corporation's general manager, William Warren, and J.H. King, the chief of the entire Wheeling Steel police force, arrived minutes later.

After an exhaustive search for the suspect came up dry, the group went over all the possible avenues of escape, including the possibility that a rowboat was used to escape to West Virginia's riverbanks. Mingo Junction police picked up a guy who had been seen jumping on a southbound train that had passed the mill around the time of the crime. The man was thirty-three-year-old Albert Yost of Wellsville. He was booked into the jail, along with twenty-nine-year-old George Otto of Steubenville. Otto was found sleeping in his car along Mingo Boulevard, by the mill fence. Brooke County authorities, who had been alerted by telephone, didn't find any suspicious persons on their side of the river.

An investigation of the murder scene revealed footprints behind the pile of bricks where the gunman waited for his prey. Police began interviewing the people who saw the shooting and those who chased the shooter. James

Stewart, who narrowly escaped death after a misfire, told police of his close encounter. "The guy turned and leveled the gun at me, but it just clicked. I don't know if it misfired or if it was empty. He ran south, toward the river." Henry Shoup, George McClymouth and John Millsop, who were all standing on the steps to the open hearth, gave statements that the gunman ran by them, waving the weapon. Martin Endich, Kenneth Hinds and Jake Schulman were all looking out of the laboratory window as the gunman dashed by them. They had received the same menacing wave.

All of the witnesses agreed that the assassin had an ape-like gait, as he waddled from side to side. They also agreed that he was short and stocky, probably middle-aged given the way he walked. He was wearing dark overalls and a matching coat. Stewart stated that he wore a black work hat with a shiny peak. "It looked like a mill policeman's hat," he provided.

Note was made of the locations of each victim. Melsheimer was killed between the cafeteria and the mill office. Barnett was killed approximately one-eighth of a mile south of that location, near the blast furnace. Kochendarfer and Messer were shot fifty feet from the open-hearth department, on the east side of the sixty-inch strip mill, which was about one hundred yards from where Melsheimer had been attacked. Kochendarfer and Messer were coworkers but didn't hang out with each other outside of work. All were killed at the same time of night. Someone mentioned that all victims were shot during a full moon, but Chief Cunningham and Sheriff Long dismissed that bit of information.

After making sure all of the witnesses knew to appear at the police station in the morning after work, law enforcement officers exited the plant. Morning was only a few hours away.

NEWS CONFERENCE

Grilling the witnesses again the next day didn't add much new information to what the cops already had. Slugs from the two latest bodies were taken by Patrolman Robert Doyle to David Cowles, the Cleveland ballistics expert. Doyle postponed his vacation to complete the task. Cunningham already knew the slugs would be a match to the previous two crimes.

At a news conference at 3:00 p.m., the chief admitted, "We're up against a blank wall." He relayed the information they had learned the night before from the interviews. "We do not know who this phantom killer is, but we do have two men in custody." A surprising development was the chief's admission that he'd had undercover officers working in the mill since the Barnett shooting. "We've got two possible motives. One motive being that we have a crazed maniac who is just shooting people at random. Our other theory is that some group is terrorizing workers to injure the reputations of the Wheeling Steel Corporation in some grudge against the company," the chief continued.

Chief Cunningham had coined the term "phantom killer." The name stuck, and from July 2 forward, the national headlines for Steubenville's mill killer would include "The Phantom." The Phantom was one of the main topics in the mill's cafeteria, where men reveled in the headline news. Some men talked loudly about the murders, while others sat in the dim corners of the cafeteria, listening, just listening.

Grave marker of Raymond Kochendarfer. *From the collection of Susan Guy.*

Grave marker of William Messer. *From the collection of Susan Guy.*

It was learned that soon after being taken to the infirmary, the bodies of the victims were transported to the McClave Funeral Home. A post-mortem had been done on them by Dr. Reed Cramer and Dr. Carl Goehring. It was determined that three slugs had hit William Messer and punctured his skin in eight places. The bullets burrowed through his arm, chest, side and shoulder. One also went through his heart and lungs. Messer, who was forty-two, was a married man with four children. He lived at 151 North High Street and had worked at the mill for two years.

Raymond Kochendarfer was hit twice. One bullet hit him in the left back side and traveled upward, striking him in the jaw. The other one hit him in the chest. Thirty-six-year-old Kochendarfer was a Washington County, Pennsylvania native and had been employed by Wheeling Steel for seven years. He and his widow, Dorothy—the wife who had kissed him goodnight a few hours earlier—had been married for twelve years. They had lost an infant daughter during that time.

Annie Messer and Dorothy Kochendarfer were taken to McClave's to identify the bodies. The grieving widows, still in shock, couldn't add anything to aid the police in their investigation. Annie Messer informed the officers, who had driven the two widows to the funeral home, that she wanted to be notified immediately after an arrest was made. Anna Kochendarfer, the mother of Ray, was working her shift at Ohio Valley Hospital when the murders happened. She met her daughter-in-law at the funeral home. The three women stayed strong, forming a unique bond. They all prayed to God for this horror at the plant to come to an end. The wives informed officials that their husbands were going to be shipped to their respective homes for burial. Kochendarfer was going to go back to Hollidaysburg, Pennsylvania, and Messer was going to be buried in his birthplace in Portsmouth, Ohio.

A BIG REWARD IS OFFERED

Two days after the double shooting, W.W. Holloway, the president of the Wheeling Steel Corporation, announced a $5,000 reward for information leading to the identity and conviction of the Phantom Killer. Jefferson County commissioners voted to up their $500 reward to $1,000. This meant the total reward was $6,000.

The two suspects picked up near the mill on the night of the murders, Albert Yost and George Otto, were questioned, but they were released after it became apparent that they had nothing to do with the crime.

Corporation officials ordered the immediate installation of powerfully bright lights to be placed in strategic locations around the mill. This was done to try to thwart the killer at his own game of hiding in the shadows to surprise his prey. The usual habit of millworkers arriving early for their shifts and loitering outside the cafeteria or around their workplaces was noticeably different. No one was loitering anywhere. The walk-with-a-buddy order was in place, and there was a totally businesslike atmosphere in the yards. Workers came and went, as expected. Safety was the first thing on everyone's mind.

The mill police force was upped to thirty men. More armed guards could be seen around the yard. Millworkers armed themselves with weapons other than firearms. Workers who had asked the police station about carrying guns were told that they'd have to be deputized to carry them. That being the case, they made their own weapons, concealing them in lunch pails and in their pockets.

PROSECUTOR HOOPER MAKES A DISCOVERY

D uring Prosecutor Arthur L. Hooper's investigation of the facts known about the Phantom Killer case, he wanted to compare the case with previous murders in Jefferson County. Per his request, his assistant, William Weinman, came up with startling information about the county's records, or rather, the county's lack of record keeping. Weinman conveyed his disturbing findings to the prosecutor. There weren't any records of murders in Jefferson County, Ohio, whether they were solved or unsolved, in the office. None of the previous prosecutors had kept such records. A subsequent search of coroner's records revealed that they, too, were woefully incomplete. Weinman went back to 1910 and compiled a list of twenty-five indictments for murder. Of the twenty-five indictments he found, five individuals were convicted of their crimes as charged, eight were acquitted, eight were convicted of lesser crimes, one pleaded guilty, two were freed by hung juries and two were marked as "no record."

Lady Justice's scales were tipping in the wrong direction, and Prosecutor Hooper was determined to level them out—at least in this case. He knew it would be a huge feather in his political cap. It could win him a run for Common Pleas Court judge in the future. He vowed that this was one case that would be solved.

He asked Weinman to continue the quest for information on past murders in Jefferson County so that it could be used for decades to come. He felt that the unsolved cases should have been kept in hopes that they could be solved someday. After all, the victims' families deserved that much.

REPORTERS WANT THE SCOOP

Newspaper reporters were clamoring for information on the Phantom Killer case. Many were hoping for a career-making story, but the information well was dry. The police and the prosecutor admitted they had nothing new to go on.

William Weinman had come up with an unsolved murder of a man in a Mingo plant years before, so Hooper decided to have that case reopened in hopes of finding a possible connection. People around the county began to recall the mysterious murders of four railroad trackmen two decades earlier. Their murders had gone unsolved. The large reward offered in the mill case prompted hundreds of rumors and pieces of false information to flood the police department. Patrolmen and investigators were wary of tracking leads down in fear of coming up with nothing. The prosecutor admitted that they were keeping a few suspects under surveillance but refused to elaborate on the statement.

In Mount Vernon, Ohio, police picked up a foreigner with a dark complexion who resembled the Steubenville Police Department's description of the mill killer. They arrested him after he had jumped off a train in the mill yards and walked into town. He admitted to Mount Vernon police that he had worked in the steel mills in Steubenville and Youngstown, but he said he was not the mill shooter. They held him until Steubenville police arrived. After a short interrogation by Steubenville officers, the man was turned loose. His long, black mustache eliminated him from their list. Their ghost shooter had no facial hair, according to a couple of witnesses, including James Stewart.

One reporter, who was anxious for a story, came up with the angle of "Moon Madness." According to him, the full moon, under which all of the shootings had been committed, had rendered the shooter a lunatic. He had become a victim of the so-called Moon Madness. Local doctors had come up with that diagnosis of the killer before the moonstruck theory was made public. While police scoffed at the idea, public opinion was shifting that way.

An unexploded .38-caliber shell was found along the fence line that separated State Route 7 and Poplar Avenue, on the west side of the mill. It was found by George Ulhich and Walter Huston, both of Steubenville. Some authorities believe it may have been dropped by the killer while he was making one of his escapes. Others dismissed it, saying it probably had no bearing on the case.

On Tuesday, July 3, two days after the double shooting, a steelworker found a raggedy, grease-stained topcoat in one of the soaking pits. It matched the description of the one the killer had worn that night in every way, except for its color. The coat was turned over to Coroner Charles Wells, who took it to the police officials. They dismissed it as not being a viable clue.

On Wednesday morning, July 4, residents from the 300 block of North Third Street walked into police headquarters with an interesting story. A short, stocky man, about five feet tall and wearing a dark gray suit, knocked on the front door of one residence. He asked the homeowner for four cents. When the homeowner refused, the man walked away and muttered, "I already killed four hunkies." He continued walking up the street.

On Friday, July 5, James Barnett, the now-crippled second victim of the phantom, gave an interview from his room at the residence of Joseph W. Miller at 128 North High Street. "That man works in the mill; I'd bet on it." The persistent Barnett had worked at the mill for almost a year. "He ran down the tracks then back into the mill. He circled back around and was in that crowd, watching me being carried to the infirmary. Why, I wouldn't be surprised if he assisted in carrying me." Barnett went on, "He knows more about that mill than I do. I'd get lost in a heartbeat if I took off running through that mill like he did. I believe he hangs around the cafeteria, then as the men are leaving, he hides. Then, he waits for his next victim. I just happened to be the unlucky one that night."

On Saturday, July 6, the first large advertisement for the $5,000 reward offered by Wheeling Steel Corporation hit the newspapers. Everyone knew it had been announced, but it was something else to see it in print. People cut it out of the paper and began snooping to see what they could dig up. Everybody wanted a piece of that reward.

$5,000 REWARD

$5,000 reward will be paid to or among the person or persons who will cause to be apprehended and convicted the person or persons who caused the death of William Messer and Ray Kochendarfer on Sunday night, July 1, 1934, at the Steubenville plant of the Wheeling Steel corporation, Steubenville, Ohio.

The president of the company will determine the person or persons and the amount of this reward to which each may be entitled.

Wheeling Steel Corporation

Reward poster that appeared in the *Steubenville Herald Star. Courtesy of the* Steubenville Herald Star.

On Friday, July 20, city, county and mill officials met to discuss a new line of investigation. They remained tight-lipped about the content of the meeting, which resulted in a flurry of rumors that the Phantom had been caught. In the few days that followed, the police station and the sheriff's department were deluged with inquiring phone calls and people coming to the station to see if this was true. The rumors went so far as to name a man who was, allegedly, placed in handcuffs in the mill yard. The man named was an employee on day shift. According to police, no such arrest record existed. The man was at work that morning in the mill.

CAPTURED

SATURDAY, JULY 28, 1934

Tips had been coming in since the Melsheimer murder on January 30. Harry "Babe" Morken, a steelworker, told authorities that night he was pretty sure that the gunman was a guy named David Dasco. Dasco was a sweeper in the new process department. That tip put Dasco on Cunningham's and Long's radar. Workers had seen him throughout the mill, in locations he had no business being in. The tips kept coming, and they all pointed to the same man. Dasco had been held and interrogated at police headquarters during the first days of the grisly shootings, after the tip from Morken. He had been released, which, in hindsight, was a costly mistake. Two more victims had died, and another was maimed for life.

The "secret" meeting that was held at the mill a few weeks earlier between county, city and mill employees was an effort to bring the case to a close. Authorities had no evidence to name David Dasco as their suspect. They had already searched the residence where he roomed after the first murder, but they came up with nothing. They needed to find the revolver. Their arrest of a suspect would be flimsy without it.

At the mill, midnight shift employees poured through the mill gates, heading to the cafeteria. It was about 11:00 p.m., and they slowly began their old routine of loitering in the cafeteria. They talked of the shootings and the loss of their three coworkers. Headlines of Dillinger had culminated in his death six days earlier, on July 22, when he was shot in an elaborate setup outside of the Biograph Theater in Chicago. Austrian chancellor Englebert Dolfuss had been assassinated on July 25 because of his hatred of the Nazis. He had been in the way of Hitler's takeover of Austria. The headlines were grim—as grim as the situation at the mill. Few talked, but many more listened.

Watching from the shadows near the mill gate, like the ghost gunner had done many times before, mill police officer John P. Fonow spied his suspect leaving the new process department, which was located near the Mingo Boulevard side of the plant. At 10:56 p.m., David Dasco made his way to the lower clock office and clocked out at 11:01 p.m. Fonow lost sight of him at that point. As Dasco continued in the direction of the cafeteria, Lieutenant Clarence "C.H." Bailey took up surveillance, while Fonow remained at his post near the gate. Bailey watched as Dasco entered the cafeteria and purchased a lunch pie. He exited the building while devouring his tasty treat. Instead of returning to the new process department, he went toward the river side of the mill, walking by the area where Melsheimer, Kochendarfer and Messer had been killed. He continued to climb a flight of stairs, leading to the pickling department. He then headed back through the open yard, to the clock office, where Fonow caught sight of him.

Twenty feet from the gate, at 11:20 p.m., Fonow stopped the strange little man as Lieutenant Bailey approached from behind. Bailey asked Dasco why he had taken a stroll around the mill. He claimed he'd lost his gloves somewhere and was looking for them. The alert Fonow noticed his suspect was clutching a pair of work gloves in his left hand. He used his hands as he talked and was waving them around all the while.

Bailey patted the protesting man down and found a Colt .38-caliber revolver in a handmade holster strapped to his leg. It was under his heavy, vastly oversized overalls. The right-hand pocket of the overalls was ripped out, allowing for easy access to the weapon.

Adrenalin pumping fast, the two men took their trophy to the mill office and called authorities. Steubenville patrolmen Sam Baker and Earl Long responded and took Dasco to the city jail, where he was put into solitary confinement. Fonow and Bailey followed, knowing they would be grilled as much as Dasco. They had, no doubt, saved someone else from becoming another victim of the phantom that night. Millworkers looked on as the suspect was driven away in the marked squad car. Paul Cash and Gilbert Porreca, the brother of city policeman Umberto Porreca, ran out of the gate and followed the car into town. Upon its arrival at the jail, they told authorities that Dasco was the man they had seen lurking around the mill for the last few days. They watched as he would hide in the shadows. After one of the murders, they had chased him until he gave them the slip.

Left: Lieutenant Clarence H. Bailey, a Wheeling Steel Mill policeman, trailed Dasco through the mill. *Courtesy of the* Steubenville Herald Star.

Right: John P. Fonow, the Wheeling Steel Mill police officer who captured the Phantom. *Courtesy of the* Steubenville Herald Star.

Shift captain Frank "Yank" Taylor questioned the suspect until top law enforcement officers arrived. Prosecutor Hooper, Sheriff Long, Chief Cunningham and Detectives Dignan and Schroeder appeared in short order. Before questioning began, Cunningham sent the revolver with Steubenville patrolman Robert Doyle and Deputy Sheriff Charles Merryman to Cleveland for ballistics testing. The chief then called Dr. C.B. Terwillegar to come to the city building to examine the prisoner.

Fonow relayed the story Dasco had told him at the mill about forgetting his gloves. "He was waving the gloves in his right hand while he was talking to me." However, a quick search of the suspect did not reveal a pair of gloves. "He must have ditched them somewhere," Fonow explained. "I know I saw them," he insisted. Dr Terwillegar's quick and unofficial examination of David Dasco showed that he suffered from dementia praecox, which was a mental disorder. Investigators had figured that their suspect would be insane.

As they had previously learned from the first time Dasco was arrested, he roomed at the Andrew and Susan Popovich home at 634½ Lincoln Avenue. He had lived there for the past two years. And five years earlier, when he moved to Steubenville from Pittsburgh and Ambridge, Pennsylvania, he lived in the 400 block of South Sixth Street. The short and stocky alleged killer's full name was David D'Ascanio. He had emigrated from Roccacasale, Aquila, Italy. He Americanized his name by shortening it to Dasco. He had come to the United States twenty-six years earlier and earned his American citizenship after enlisting in the U.S. Army. He served in Company M, Sixth Infantry, during the World War. He spent fourteen days in the trenches and claimed to have been wounded at Meuse-Argonne. He was a bachelor and had two brothers still living in Italy.

"I no shoot nobody," Dasco mumbled. "I no shoot nobody." The man kept repeating the sentence in his low, broken English. "I don't talk, I live. I talk, I die," was another statement he repeated over and over, as the room full of seasoned lawmen tried, in frustration, to break him down. He was grilled throughout the night.

In the early morning hours of July 29, Dasco was transferred to the Jefferson County Jail and placed in solitary confinement on the second tier, for safety reasons. He was stripped of his clothing, and his belt was not given back to him for fear he might try to hang himself. Armed deputies were placed inside and outside the jail. Loiterers were shooed away with the help of city police. Law enforcement's fear of an angry mob wanting to get their hands on the object of their recent nightmares did not come to fruition. Citizens and millworkers seemed to be satisfied that he was caught and heaved a collective sigh of relief.

Questioning resumed later in the morning, with the prisoner still proclaiming his innocence. When asked about the gun, Dasco answered, "I buy gun four or five days ago for seventy-five cents, from some guy on North High Street when I went to get a drink from the natural spring at the pothouse. I buy gun for protection. Why I shoot anybody? I no shoot nobody." The sheriff realized the "pothouse" mentioned by Dasco referred to Ohio Valley Clay. The Italian sweeper in the new process department, still covered in soot from working at the mill the day before, was clutching the top of his beltless, oversized overalls and shifting from one foot to the other. Shoulders hunched, he began to answer their questions more freely, stating he had no friends. "You got to have money to have friends. I got no money; I just work in mill. All time."

Lawmen exited the cell and looked back as Dasco sat down on his cot. Sheriff Long clanged the cell door shut, the noisy tumblers creaking as he turned the key. He glanced at the prisoner, marveling at the resemblance he bore to Giuseppe Zangara, the assassin of Chicago mayor Anton Cermak.

David Dasco's mugshot. *From the collection of Susan Guy.*

"It's really uncanny," he muttered under his breath. As Dasco sank into a prone position on the cot, with hands behind his head, he inquired, in a matter-of-fact manner, "When we eat?"

At the time Dasco was being questioned, Chief Cunningham, along with Patrolmen Sam Baker and David Lyle, drove over to the Popovich residence on Lincoln Avenue. They were accompanied by a couple of county deputies. Though they had searched the room and the entire residence previously, they needed to search it again. A successful prosecution of the case depended on what they found.

Upon entering Dasco's room, the lawmen noticed the keyhole of his door had been plugged with paper. Crime magazines and newspapers from Steubenville, Wheeling and Pittsburgh were found in his drawers, under rugs and under the mattress. They pulled down the window blind and realized it was a double blind made of heavy mill paper. In between the blinds were articles cut out of newspapers about the attempted assassination of President Franklin D. Roosevelt in 1933, before his inauguration. This attempt by gunman Giuseppe "Joe" Zangara killed Chicago mayor Anton Cermak instead. The lawmen marveled at Zangara's resemblance to Dasco. A large picture of Zangara was found on the blind. Dasco's fascination with crime and criminals was undeniable. Clothing that was found in his room closely matched the outfit worn by the killer. A grotesque-looking, black, hand-sewn mask and hat—like those the mill police wore—was found among Dasco's belongings in a dresser. A search of the other drawers revealed strange hoardings of paper sacks, bags of nails, wooden blocks and other pieces of wood. The same was found in suitcases and piles on the floor. They also found a will, bequeathing one thousand lire to Dasco's brother in Italy—equivalent to fifty-seven cents in U.S. currency. The gracefulness of the handwriting was noted by the investigators. The will had been written in both Italian and English. Dasco had a notable collection of movie and crime magazines as well.

Susan Popovich, the landlady, and James Clarke, another Popovich tenant, informed the lawmen that any time David Dasco went to the bathroom, he would lock his door. The bathroom was only fifteen feet away. Mrs. Popovich said he would lock the door any time he was not there. He had bawled her out once when she had cleaned his room. He noticed things had been rearranged and lost his temper. He ordered her to stay out of his room. Mrs. Popovich, whose husband, Andrew, was an invalid, needed the rent money, so she abided by Dasco's wishes instead of throwing him out. James Clarke stated that David Dasco never ate his meals at the rooming house. He had a daily habit of sitting on the wall at Beatty Park, which was just across the street from the Popovich home. Kids often made fun of him there because of his odd, ape-like walk, but he always appeared to ignore them. Clarke said he'd seen Dasco doing a ritual at the Beatty Park flagpole. The man was so strong, he could grab the flagpole with both hands and suspend his body sideways, in mid-air, for about three minutes at a time. He would do that every day. Cunningham raised his eyebrows when he heard of the unusual feat.

After they left the Popovich residence, Cunningham sent Detectives Tom Dignan and Ernest Schroeder to all of the pawn shops and firearms dealers in Steubenville. While Cleveland ballistics experts tried to determine the year that the murderer's gun was manufactured and trace its ownership trail, the detectives tried to determine how Dasco ended up with it.

Their search led them to a pawn shop by the mill gate. The owner, Louis Rosansky, was questioned about the sale of any revolvers in the last six months; then, he was taken to the jail, where he viewed Dasco. The detectives had the prisoner walk back and forth in his cell. Rosansky watched him move. "Yes, he seems very familiar to me." The pawn shop owner reflected for a moment. He recalled selling a revolver in January to a man who reminded him of Dasco. "Yes, I believe that is the guy." The acknowledgement made the detectives very happy.

In the late afternoon, Prosecutor Hooper began a parade of the witnesses who had come closest to the mill killer. Those persons included Harry Morken, Paul Cash, Gil Porreca, James Stewart and James Barnett. Most of them identified David Dasco as the man they saw fleeing from the crimes. However, James Barnett, his only living victim, wasn't sure if Dasco was his assailant. The prosecutor was happy with the few confirmations he got—tomorrow was another day.

15

ARRAIGNMENT AND INDICTMENT

O n July 30, after Prosecutor Hooper shot down rumors that a death list, containing the names of ten men, was found on the alleged shooter, a new batch of witnesses, led by Hooper, was paraded through the jail. Among these witnesses was Mrs. William Messer, a widow of one of the victims. Annie Messer, who was accompanied by her oldest son, Charles, walked up to the cell door, her unblinking gaze staying on Dasco. This made the prisoner visibly uncomfortable; his head lowered, and his eyes stared at the concrete floor. The courageous widow spoke directly to Dasco, "Why did you do it? Can you tell me that? He was my husband; he was the father of our four children."

The little Italian man never looked up and didn't answer her. Charles, who was the spitting image of his father, stepped up to the bars of the cold cell. His voice, quivering with a rising anger, took up where his mother's had left off. "You can't answer my mother? You had no right to take my father's life! You know you did it; why don't you confess?" His mother stood silently by as her son's rage took hold. He was entitled to show that rage, after all. He took his father's death very hard. Twenty-year-old Charles was a steelworker at the same mill, and he remembered David Dasco from the new process department. He remembered the creepy little guy who was always lurking in places that he didn't belong. Millworkers talked, and he'd heard the rumors and wondered if this guy was his father's killer. Now, there he was, facing Dasco in a jail cell. Charles was sober at the time, because he knew he had a mission to accomplish that day with his poor mother, but alcohol flowed through his veins daily in those days. It helped him deal with the sudden loss of a father he had viewed as a hero. Now, there was his killer, cold as ice, not giving them the answers they needed to go on. Dasco looked at the young man and stated, clearly, "I no shoot nobody." That was his standard reply, and he was sticking to it.

Mrs. Messer asked the prosecutor if she could have Dasco turn from side to side and walk across the cell. Hooper ordered the prisoner to do as Mrs. Messer requested. She watched every movement, then asked to leave. When they got outside the cell area and out of earshot of Dasco, the widow stopped. "Mr. Hooper," Anna Messer spoke up, "the day before Bill was killed, a man was lurking around outside our residence. He just stood on the sidewalk out front and stared at the house. I believe that he is the same man that you have locked up in there." She went on. "He was wearing gray, pinstriped pants, a gray shirt and one of those white, straw Panama hats." Hooper took down her statement and thanked the helpful duo. After escorting them to the door, he had investigators return to the Popovich home to search for the clothing and the all-important hat. Within the hour, a triumphant Dignan and Schroeder returned with the incriminating clothing and a white, straw Panama hat. The evidence was mounting.

On Tuesday, July 31, David Cowles, the ballistics expert in Cleveland, called Prosecutor Hooper's office with great news. The Colt .38-caliber revolver they took from David D'Ascanio—alias David Dasco—was the same weapon that had killed Fred Melsheimer, Ray Kochendarfer and William Messer. It had also maimed James Barnett. The ecstatic prosecutor almost danced a jig at the long-awaited news. He needed to get Dasco indicted. Common Pleas Court judge Jay S. Paisley told Hooper that he would sign an entry to have the grand jury recalled. He suggested the prosecutor have a commission of doctors give the prisoner a sanity hearing. Prosecutor Hooper informed Judge Paisley that a sanity hearing would be done after the indictment from the grand jury.

Prosecutor Arthur L. Hooper prepared the affidavit to file formal charges of first-degree murder against David D'Ascanio. In a last-ditch effort to get the man to talk, investigators grilled him from 4:00 p.m. the day before to the early hours of the next morning. His only statement was, "If I talk, I die; if I don't talk, I live." Bewildered by that statement, officials tried, in vain, to find out what he meant by it. Even after he was told of the likelihood that he would go to the electric chair, Dasco remained unfazed. He protested his innocence and never wavered.

COLT .38 POLICE SPECIAL

Artist's rendering of the Colt .38-caliber revolver used by David Dasco in the mill murders. *Courtesy of artist Jimmy Bee.*

As Hooper prepared the affidavit, investigators were sent to Wells Street to search for items that may have been discarded there by Dasco. Nothing was found as they continued into the large sewer pipe that ran from Fisher's Run, under the mill. The pipe carried water from the stream to the Ohio River and was less than three hundred yards from the Popovich home. It was Dasco's probable escape route after the murders. The search was fruitless.

The next step was to search for money that Dasco may have hidden, banked or sent to his two brothers in Italy. He had kept meticulous records of his rent receipts and money he had sent to his brother. He denied having any money, though he had been employed at the mill for years. The prosecutor asked if he wished to retain an attorney. Dasco replied, "I got no money to recompense them."

Due to Judge Randall Buchanan's absence, the arraignment was postponed. The judge was on a well-deserved vacation in Vermont. On Wednesday, August 1, Attorney Thomas Rock went to the jail to talk to Dasco. He was stopped by Sheriff Long, who asked if he was Dasco's attorney. Rock replied, "Not yet, but he sent for me. Simon Carpino and I will be representing him from here on out." The sheriff instructed, "Come back in an hour." After Rock's departure, Sheriff Long ordered a bath and a shave for the scroungy prisoner. He was given gray slacks and a light gray shirt to wear. His fresh, clean appearance made him look totally different. The clothes and bath seemed to give D'Ascanio an air of confidence. He loosened up a bit. The sheriff asked him how he felt. Dasco replied, "I feel pretty good now. I got good night's sleep." He went on, in broken English, "I just feel upset yesterday."

With Prosecutor Hooper filing affidavits for three first-degree, premeditated murder charges against him, Dasco finally hired a defense counsel. Attorneys Thomas Rock and Simon Carpino were well-known, competent lawyers in Jefferson County.

It had been announced that the arraignment would take place sometime on Friday, August 3, before Judge Buchanan. Dasco's defense attorneys planned to demand a preliminary hearing at the arraignment, in an effort to learn what kind of evidence the state had against their client. The state planned to call two witnesses at the arraignment, Lieutenant C.H. Bailey and special mill police officer John P. Fonow, the two men who had arrested Dasco at the mill gate. Dasco's defense counsel declared that they would demand the state release some of the evidence. They issued a statement to the press that David D'Ascanio's arrest was a mistake.

Prosecutor Hooper changed his plans of having Judge Paisley recall the grand jury. He would, instead, wait for the September term of the grand jury. This new strategy would allow Hooper to not rush the investigation. Extremely aware of how Rock and Carpino operated in the courtroom, Hooper did not want to give any perception that their defendant was being "railroaded" by the prosecution.

Shortly before 2:00 p.m. on Friday, August 3, Sheriff Ray Long and two of his deputies whisked the little Italian from his cell on the top floor of the county jail to a waiting squad card in the alley. The county jail was surrounded by a large crowd of curious onlookers who were hoping to catch a glimpse of the infamous Phantom who had thrust their city, once again, into the national spotlight. The crowd parted, allowing the lawmen and their handcuffed prisoner to proceed freely to the squad car. Once inside the car, they sped north on Court Street to Washington Street, turning down Third Street. As they pulled up to the side entrance of the city building, they were met by Captain Ed Nolan and six Steubenville patrolmen, who formed a cordon around Dasco. They escorted him into the city building. They finally reached the courtroom, after passing through a crowd of two hundred people who had anxiously gathered for the arraignment proceedings.

Dasco was dressed in his gray shirt and gray pinstriped pants; it was a sharp contrast from the man in oversized overalls and a black cap that people had seen in the newspapers. The clean-shaven, well-kempt, quiet little man in well-fitting clothes did not look like a crazed gunman. He was seated at a table in the middle of the courtroom and was left alone for about four minutes while lawmen took their places in various spots inside and outside of the building. The crowd outside was peering into the rear windows, hoping to get a peek at the man, and the crowd inside grew silent.

Judge Randall Buchanan entered the room and took the bench. He only looked at one affidavit that day—that of victim Fred Melsheimer. He instructed his clerk, George Floto, to swear in the witnesses. There were five witnesses for the state: Lieutenant Marshall Jack and Patrolman Fred Teaff of the Steubenville Police Department, Coroner Charles Wells and mill police officers Lieutenant C.H. Bailey and Patrolman John P. Fonow. Defense

Judge Randall Buchanan presided over David Dasco's arraignment. *From the collection of Susan Guy.*

Attorney Thomas Rock, on behalf of his client, waived the reading of the charges. Coroner Wells was the first witness to take the stand. He relayed to the judge that he had been called to the mill on the night of January 30 to do a quick examination of the body; he said he had taken one of the two slugs from the body of Fred Melsheimer.

Lieutenant Bailey described how he had followed Dasco after he'd punched out at the clock office and went to the cafeteria for a pie. Instead of exiting the mill, Bailey said Dasco passed by where each victim had been gunned down and weaved through various parts of the mill. Lieutenant Bailey said that, at some point, Dasco must have realized he was being followed, because he headed back toward the gate. It was at that point that Bailey asked Dasco to stop. Officer Fonow, who was waiting nearby, closed in on the man. Bailey went on to say that a search of the suspect revealed the canvas holster strapped to Dasco's leg that held the .38-caliber revolver. He described the man's oversized overalls with the pocket cut out so that he could easily draw the weapon. Bailey ended his testimony by saying, "The city police were called, and Dasco was turned over to them."

Upon cross-examination of Lieutenant Bailey, and with no defense witnesses in his corner, Dasco's attorney, Thomas Rock, seized his opportunity to pounce. "Lieutenant Bailey, while you were at the police station, didn't you observe Mr. Dasco being beaten to obtain a confession?"

"No, sir, not to my knowledge," Bailey replied.

Attorney Rock proceeded with his line of questioning. "You didn't hear anything about this, but the people who live across the alley heard this man yell?"

"No, sir, I did not," Bailey stated.

Rock walked over to the defendant's chair and led Dasco over to where Lieutenant Bailey was sitting. Pulling up Dasco's trousers, he exposed his legs, which were covered in red welts and cuts. Bailey denied any knowledge of how the injuries got there.

Prosecutor Arthur Hooper watched the display going on in front of him. He knew how Tom Rock played the game of law. The guy was good at getting his clients acquitted—though his methods were questionable. Hooper knew he'd never want to play poker with the guy, but then, sometimes, the game was about who held the right cards. Hooper knew he was holding the right cards. He had the winning hand.

Rock continued grilling Lieutenant Bailey. "Isn't it true you're testifying this way so you and Officer Fonow can collect some of the reward money?"

"No," was Bailey's reply.

Rock shot back with, "You mean you're not?"

"If Dasco is guilty, yes," Bailey replied.

"Do you think he's guilty?"

Bailey answered, "I don't know."

The next witness, Lieutenant Marshall Jack, testified that he took the slugs from the mill and turned them over to Patrolman Frank Teaff, the city's ballistics officer. Teaff took his turn on the stand, testifying to the similarity of the bullets taken from Melsheimer's body on January 30 and the one taken from James Barnett on March 25. Thomas Rock demanded to see the bullets at once. After demanding, again, to see the slugs, Patrolman Teaff told him that the bullets were not in his possession. The prosecutor stood, advising Attorney Rock that the bullets were in Cleveland at the ballistics lab.

Mill police chief William McCloskey took the stand in place of Officer Fonow and produced David Dasco's timecard for January 30. The timecard revealed that Dasco had punched in at 2:00 p.m., then out again at 4:01 p.m. He returned to the mill that night, punching in at 10:00 p.m., and he punched out a few minutes after midnight.

After McCloskey's testimony was finished, Prosecutor Hooper advised that the state rested. Rock had no witnesses. Judge Buchanan declared that the state had shown probable cause, and he bound Dasco over to the grand jury without bond.

Sheriff Long and his deputies scurried Dasco back through the crowd to the waiting cruiser and made their return to the Jefferson County Jail. David D'Ascanio remained there until the September term of the grand jury came in. They would determine if he should be indicted for first-degree murder for the death of Fred Melsheimer.

Per Judge Jay Paisley's earlier request—and the prosecutor's promise—Dr. Harry Hyde, the supervisor of the State Asylum at Massillon, arrived to examine Dasco's mental state. Dr. Hyde was a widely known specialist who often testified in psychopathic cases. Sheriff Long escorted the doctor to Dasco's cell, where the prisoner refused to talk unless his attorneys were present. After Rock and Carpino found out about Dr. Hyde's presence at the jail, they put a stop to his examination for a time. It resumed after the two attorneys were granted permission to observe. Hooper stayed in the room with them. After talking at length with the prisoner, Dr. Hyde gave him a physical examination. He advised Hooper that he would notify him later of his findings, then left for Massillon.

It was a waiting game for Dasco until September. He had plenty of time to rest, but city and county lawmen did not. They were still busy with all the other crimes and trials going on in their jurisdiction.

16

THE GRAND JURY

The convening of the September term of the grand jury took place on September 10, with Judge J.C. Oglevee presiding. Judge Oglevee had stepped in for Judge Jay S. Paisley, who was suffering from an illness. Witnesses began giving testimony; among them was Cleveland ballistics expert David Cowles. Cowles testified to his belief that the slugs from all three murders and the wounding of James Barnett were fired from the same gun.

The evidence in all three murder cases was heard by the grand jury. On Tuesday, September 18, escorted by Prosecutor Hooper, the grand jury visited the Wheeling Steel Steubenville Plant. There, they were able to view, firsthand, the locations of the three shootings and the possible escape routes used by the phantom gunman. They also viewed Dasco's circuitous route through the plant, led by Lieutenant C.H. Bailey. The crime scene visit concluded with the site of Dasco's capture at the front gate. The grand jury had everything they needed to deliver a verdict. They exited the Wheeling Steel Plant and headed back to the courthouse.

The next morning, the grand jury came back with three murder indictments on the phantom gunman of the mill. Thomas Rock and Simon Carpino represented Dasco in the trial for his life. According to reports in the *Steubenville Herald Star*, it was learned that Dasco's fellow Italian countrymen from McKeesport, Pennsylvania, where he had lived for a short time, were taking up money for his defense fund.

At 9:45 a.m. on Monday, September 24, David D'Ascanio—alias Dasco—was escorted into the overcrowded courtroom by Deputy John Kirk. Judge

J.C. Oglevee presided over the arraignment. Defense attorney Thomas Rock waived the reading of the three first-degree murder indictments and entered a "not guilty" plea for his client. Judge Oglevee, however, insisted on the reading of the indictments. They were read to Dasco by clerk Kenneth Cavanaugh. Dasco listened as he read each indictment and gave a "not guilty" plea to each one. With his graceful penmanship, despite shackled hands, Dasco signed each indictment. Prosecutor Hooper announced he would use the Ray Kochendarfer indictment for trial, saving the other two indictments in case he needed them.

As per procedure, Judge Oglevee issued a special venire to Sheriff Ray Long for seventy-five jurors. As soon as the sheriff assembled his prospective jurors, the law required that fifteen days lapsed before the trial began. Then, three days before the trial, Dasco was given a copy of the list of potential jurors so that he and his attorneys could examine it. It probably took two days to seat a jury, and the trial was expected to take a week, as the prosecutor had a long list of witnesses.

On October 12, defense attorney Rock made a motion to examine the alleged murder weapon and the slugs taken from Kochendarfer. His motion was granted by Judge Oglevee. Rock also made a motion to obtain the bullets that were allegedly fired from Lieutenant Marshall Jack's revolver, in order to compare them with the murder slugs. Rock's motion included bullets from all three victims. Hooper argued that he was only trying the case of Ray Kochendarfer and that evidence from the other two cases shouldn't be involved. Hooper concluded from Rock and Carpino's slick move that they intended to refute the ballistics testimony of David Cowles. The prosecutor expected nothing less from his courtroom opponent. Rock bellowed, "This is a highly publicized case. My client is being accused over and over on the front page of every paper in the country of being the Phantom Killer. I have every right to examine the slugs in every case. He's being accused of every case, and we will deny each one!"

The prosecutor reluctantly agreed to turn over the slugs for all the victims. As for slugs from the gun of Lieutenant Marshall Jack, he replied, "I don't know anything about that. If you can find those, you can examine them."

Following their verbal exchange, Rock addressed reporters. "I promise you, there will plenty of ballistics at the trial." Prosecutor Hooper's reply to the reporters was, "I have witnesses who will testify that they saw Dasco before July with a gun on mill property. I'm not just relying on ballistics." Hooper walked out of the courthouse, noting that the verbal poker game had begun.

On Monday, October 15, one week before the trial, Attorneys Thomas Rock and Simon Carpino requested that Judge Oglevee appoint them as counsel for David D'Ascanio. Their client could not afford their services for the lengthy murder trial. If they were court-appointed counsel, the county would pay for their client's defense. Prosecutor Hooper, who was present at the time of the request, had no objection. Rock stated his reason for the request. "We've spent over $500, and, to date, we've only received $365." The judge advised that he would let them know his decision in the morning but reserved the right to choose his own counsel. On Tuesday morning, Judge Oglevee met with Rock, Carpino and Prosecutor Hooper. Attorney Peter A. Gavin was also in the room. "I've made my decision," the judge began, "which is to appoint Thomas Rock and P.A. Gavin as defense counsel for Mr. D'Ascanio." After some objection from Rock and Carpino, it was determined that Carpino could stay on the case and work independently; that would be his choice to do so. Rock and Gavin would be paid by the county.

The trial was coming up very soon, so the prosecutor and his first assistant, Harry Chalfant, began getting their exhibits together, while the defense stayed mum on their strategy.

17

LAW ENFORCEMENT STAYS BUSY

As David D'Ascanio sat in the county jail, awaiting his trial, law enforcement in Jefferson County was not sitting back, twiddling its thumbs. On September 24, Steubenville's alleged mob boss and two other men were taken to the Ohio Valley Hospital with gunshots after an unexplained fight broke out in Steubenville, at Seventh and Kilgore Streets. Jimmy Tripodi, the "mob boss" and main supplier of bootleg liquor in the area, was shot by Sam Saggio of Yorkville. A couple of other men were also shot—one man's teeth were shot out. Tripodi was shot above the knee. Saggio was beaten up by a mob. Tripodi was under guard at the hospital; no charges were filed against him. Sam Saggio was taken to the city jail with a badly lacerated face.

Governor White issued a statewide ban on all types of gambling, including slot machines. This prompted Mayor McMaster to order the police department to crack down on establishments known to be hot gambling spots. Two Steubenville police officers ignored the order and faced suspension.

One of Ohio's biggest news stories at the time was the attempted prison break at the Ohio Penitentiary in September. Harry Pierpont, Charles Makley and Russell Clark, the men convicted of the death of Allen County sheriff Jess Sarber, after they had already broken the late John Dillinger out of jail there, attempted to escape death row by using guns carved from soap. After feigning an illness, Pierpont grabbed the keys from the guard who had brought him his meal. He then unlocked the cells of everyone on death row, including Russell Clark and Charles Makley. So, all of the death row inmates were standing in the cage. Eight guards responded after getting the alert from L-block. They rushed in and started firing their weapons. Makley and Pierpont were hit and went down. All of the other death row inmates, including Russell Clark, returned to their cells. Charles Makley died of his wounds.

After public enemy no. 1, John Dillinger, had been killed on July 24, the DOI (Division of Investigation) named its next public enemy no. 1: Charles "Pretty Boy" Floyd, another ruthless, bank-robbing cop killer. Jefferson County sheriff Ray B. Long and his men were on the lookout for Floyd. The sheriff knew that Floyd's right-hand man, Adam Richetti, had a coalminer brother named David living in Dillonvale. Floyd and Richetti were known to have holed up at his home there. Public enemy no. 1 was allegedly heading for Jefferson County, and Midwest authorities were on the hunt for him.

At the national level, the Bruno Hauptmann trial had started. Bruno was on trial for kidnapping the son of famed aviator Charles Lindbergh. Those headlines were both huge, but the Phantom Killer of Steubenville, Ohio, rivaled them all. The buzz in the Wheeling Steel cafeteria was mainly about the Phantom's upcoming trial. He topped all talk of the gangsters, bank robbers, kidnappers and jailbreakers. Did Dasco accomplish what he had set out to do? A motive for his crime could not be determined by local law enforcement. Motive or not, the infamy and headlines of Dasco rivaled that of the late Dillinger. And, yes, it even rivaled the assassination attempt of President-elect Roosevelt by fellow Italian countryman Giuseppe Zangara— the man he was compared to by local lawmen, the man whose photograph had hung in his room.

18

PUBLIC ENEMY NO. 1 SPOTTED IN JEFFERSON COUNTY, OHIO

OCTOBER 21, 1934

L aw enforcement, David Dasco, millworkers and the nation were nervously awaiting the Phantom Killer's trial that was going to take place the next day. On this morning, that would turn out to be the last thing on Jefferson County sheriff Ray Bliss Long's mind. A prisoner at the jail in Wellsville, in Columbiana County, Ohio, twenty miles north of Steubenville, refused to give the police his name. Sheriff Long, accompanied by deputies and members of the Steubenville Police Department, arrived at the jail to join the posse, hunting for the man's alleged partner.

Long recognized the prisoner as Adam Richetti, Pretty Boy Floyd's right-hand man. They knew they were on a manhunt for public enemy no. 1. As law enforcement from other states and federal agents arrived in Wellsville, the police chief there refused to turn over Richetti to any of them.

The headlines of Ohio newspapers on the capture of Richetti and the one-hundred-man posse looking for Pretty Boy Floyd were huge. Right beside their photographs on the front page of the *Steubenville Herald Star* was a photograph of the Phantom Killer. He had made it to the big time. The next day—the day of the much-awaited trial—Pretty Boy Floyd stole the headlines, as he met his death in a shootout in Wellsville.

Charles Arthur "Pretty Boy" Floyd, public enemy no. 1 of the FBI, mugshot. *Public domain.*

19

THE TRIAL

The long-awaited trial day had finally arrived. Court convened promptly at 9:30 a.m., with Judge J.C. Oglevee out of Carroll County, Ohio, presiding over the trial. He was filling in for a still-ailing Judge Jay S. Paisley. Judge Oglevee's first order of business was to sign the order appointing Attorneys Thomas Rock and Peter A. Gavin as counsel for the defendant. Simon Carpino, the associate of Thomas Rock, would remain on the case independently as a third attorney. All of the men involved in the trial, including Prosecutor Arthur Hooper, signed the order.

An unshackled Dasco was then escorted into the courtroom by Sheriff Long. He had given himself a haircut in his cell the night before. His attire consisted of a gray suit, a white shirt, a dark green tie and black shoes. The sheriff seated the man behind his attorneys. The courtroom had standing room only. Approximately 350 people had crowded inside to view the trial.

Next on the judge's list was to have clerk Kenneth Cavanaugh call the list of seventy-five veniremen (or prospective jurors). The veniremen stood and took their place next to the judge's bench as their seats in the gallery were quickly snatched by curious onlookers. The judge instructed them all not to speak about the case and excused them to await call.

Deputies were ordered by Judge Oglevee to close and guard all doors of the courtroom and refuse entry to any further curiosity seekers. The process of jury selection had begun. By noon, eleven of the seventy people who had shown up had been examined by both the prosecution and defense. Out of those eleven, there were four persons tentatively seated for the jury.

The first juror seated was Hattie Nunley, who ran a hotel in Yorkville at the southern end of the county. Mrs. Nunley, a respected citizen of Yorkville, was a member of the school board. The second juror picked was Mrs. Margaret George, who was a niece of Sheriff Ray B. Long. After stating that she opposed capital punishment, Mrs. George assumed that she would be let go as a juror, but in a surprising move, defense attorney Rock kept her on the jury. The third and fourth jurors were A.C. Riffle of Toronto and Sue M. Diest, a housewife who lived in Steubenville. Court recessed at noon and reconvened again at 1:30 p.m.

Mrs. Edith Elswick of Steubenville was the next potential juror to be called. Challenged by the defense for having allegedly formed a preconceived opinion of the defendant's guilt or innocence, they accepted her, after the court disallowed the challenge. Mrs. Elswick was the daughter of former Jefferson County sheriff Western T. Baker.

The sixth juror seated was L.A. Black, a sewer pipe worker from Irondale. By 3:30 p.m., five more jurors had been seated: Ethel McElroy of Wintersville, Mrs. Sue Brown of Steubenville, Clarence Patton of Bergholz, Arnold Adey and Mrs. Robert F. Quinn of Steubenville. With court adjourned for the day, everyone was advised to be back in the courtroom by 9:00 a.m. to complete the jury selection process.

On October 23, just before 9:00 a.m., David Dasco was led to the defense table and seated next to his attorneys. The well-kempt man appeared to be in a good mood as he conversed with Rock, Gavin and Carpino. Judge Oglevee appeared promptly, convening court for the day. The jury selection began with defense attorney Rock using his second peremptory challenge to remove Sue Brown from the jury. She was replaced by Reuben Hall of Rayland. Mrs. Quinn was dismissed, as was Catherine Roe, the widow of murdered Steubenville police lieutenant Scott Roe. Prosecutor Hooper, it was alleged, was using his peremptory challenges to lessen the number of women on the jury, as they were known to be more sympathetic when it came to condemning prisoners to death.

At 10:20 a.m., both sides agreed to the jurors they had seated, including the thirteenth juror, who was to be used if one of the other jurors became ill or had to be dismissed. The final list of jurors that determined the fate of Steubenville's Phantom was as follows: Mrs. Hattie Nunley, proprietor of the Nunley Hotel in Yorkville; Mrs. Sue M. Diest, a clerk who lived at 419 Lawson Avenue; L.A. Black, a sewer worker from Irondale; Miss Ethel McElroy, a housekeeper from Steubenville; Clarence Patton, a farmer from Bergholz; Arnold Adey, an electrician from Rural Route 1 in Steubenville; Reuben

Hall, a miner from Rayland; Richard Gault, a black barber from Coal Hill; George Devlin, a miner from Alikanna; Alonzo K. McCue, a carpenter who lived at 2234 Sunset Boulevard; Mrs. A.N. Powell, a housewife from Rural Route 2 in Steubenville; and Mrs. Malinda A. Guy, a black woman from Steubenville. Matt Friend, an unemployed man from Toronto, was selected as the thirteenth juror. Forty of the veniremen had been examined before the final thirteen were chosen. After giving instructions to the jury, the remainder of the venire were dismissed and were not required to return.

Prosecutor Hooper made a motion that the jurors be allowed to view the crime scene; it was a motion that the defense attorneys concurred with. The judge ordered court bailiff William Fellows to take the jury to Wheeling Steel later in the afternoon and reminded the jury to not discuss the case with anyone. Judge Oglevee administered the oath to Bailiff Fellows, which legally placed the jury in his custody. The judge informed the jurors that they were not to separate while at the mill.

At 1:00 p.m., on Tuesday, October 23, a bus arrived at the courthouse to take the judge, attorneys, jurors and newspaper reporters to the mill. A handcuffed David Dasco was permitted to accompany the group to the site of his alleged crimes. He was brought to the mill by Sheriff Long and two deputies, Joseph Morrow and Cyrus Cook. The bus was followed closely by the sheriff's car and arrived at Wheeling Steel Corporation's front gate at 1:30 p.m. The bus was met by mill police chief William McCloskey; J.H. King, the superintendent of the Wheeling Steel police force; and Lieutenant C.H. Bailey, one of Dasco's captors. Bailey guided the tour, taking the jurors and others from the clock office where Dasco had punched out, through the mill and into the cafeteria. Curious millworkers lined doorways and windows and stopped in their tracks to watch as the group toured the various scenes. Bailey explained how he and Fonow had trailed Dasco through the mill. Some members in the group heard Dasco deny some of Bailey's accounts to his lawyers.

Along the route, Prosecutor Hooper pointed out the shooting sites of James Barnett and Fred Melsheimer, even though he was only trying the Kochendarfer case. That move took a few people on the tour by surprise. Fred Melsheimer was killed a few feet from the entrance to the number three strip mill. A bullet hole from that night was pointed out to the jury. The Barnett shooting site was visited next. The only living victim of the Phantom had been walking up a set of steps that led to a changing shack when he was attacked. The shack was adjacent to Poplar Avenue. When the group reached the spot where Kochendarfer and Messer had met their fate, near the open-hearth department, the prosecutor pointed out a stack of barrels where the gunman had concealed himself. The jurors were asked to focus their attention on this area, as it was pertinent to the case that they would be hearing. Two iron pegs, which were driven into the ground about thirty feet from the open hearth, marked the spots where the two victims were standing on the night of July 1. Buildings, lights and other areas of interest were pointed out to the jurors; among them was the laboratory where James Stewart was confronted by the shooter, only to be saved by a misfire.

That concluded the tour of the crime scene, and everyone climbed aboard the bus except for the shackled Dasco and his uniformed escorts, who got into the squad car. All parties arrived back at the courthouse, taking their respective places in the packed courtroom. Judge Oglevee took his place on the bench and called court in session; however, due to a recommendation from the court, it was decided to postpone the opening statements until Wednesday morning. The crowd of onlookers, who had waited all afternoon for the opening statements, left disappointed as Judge Oglevee adjourned court for the day. He gave instructions for the jury to go directly to their hotel and to be back in court at 9:00 a.m.

The next morning, a throng of people pushed and shoved their way into the courtroom, attempting to get a seat for the start of the most anticipated trial in Steubenville history. The Phantom Killer of Steubenville was in for the fight of his life over the murder of Ray Kochendarfer. Judge Oglevee declared that court was in session at 9:00 a.m. The room was deathly silent as Prosecutor Hooper began his opening statement by reading a copy of the indictment. "The question for your consideration is to determine whether, on July 1, 1934, David Dasco killed Ray Kochendarfer of Steubenville." He continued by describing various locations in the mill, the shooting of the two men and the escape of the killer, who made his getaway at a dogtrot not a full-out run. The prosecutor's opening statement lasted for one hour and forty minutes and outlined his numerous witnesses and what they had seen. He ended his speech by requesting that the jury find Dasco guilty of first-degree murder without the recommendation of mercy. This would mean that Dasco would die in the electric chair.

Then, defense attorney P.A. Gavin gave his opening statement, which lasted for a total of five minutes. "David D'Ascanio, or Dasco, is not the Phantom Killer of the mill yards. You will learn of the history of this man." He began, "It will be brought out that he and the victim, Ray Kochendarfer, were strangers. There was no motive for Dasco to kill him." At the conclusion of the opening statements, the state's witnesses were sworn in. They were then removed from the courtroom under the custody of Bailiff William Fellows.

Two Cleveland newspapermen arrived with a request to take photographs. Judge Oglevee and Judge Jay Paisley, who was in the courtroom, conferred. They granted permission for the photographs to be taken, at which time, the placement of the photography lights began.

For a man whose life hung in the balance, Dasco seemed to enjoy all the attention his trial was attracting. He, along with his team of court-appointed attorneys, smiled for the cameras. Photographs were also taken of the two judges, the press table and the huge crowd that lined the walls of the courtroom.

After the Cleveland reporters removed their equipment, the proceedings began, and the state called its first witness, Coroner Charles R. Wells. Wells was one of the first people to arrive at the plant on the night that Kochendarfer and Messer were killed, and he was one of the first to view the bodies. He accompanied the bodies to the funeral home, where he observed Dr. Goehring remove two bullets from Kochendarfer's body. One bullet was removed from his chest, the other from his mouth, where it had lodged. Wells advised that he personally took both bullets and turned them over to Prosecutor Hooper. Upon cross-examination by Attorney Rock, Wells stated that no bullets had been removed from the body of William Messer.

Dr. Carl Goehring was the next witness to take the stand. He had performed the autopsy on Kochendarfer and stated that the victim had died of hemorrhaging of the lungs and heart as a result of the gunshot wounds. When shown two slugs, he identified them as the bullets he'd removed from the victim's body. They were offered as the state's exhibit number one. The defense did not object to the move, and Goehring was dismissed.

Dorothy Kochendarfer, the widow of one of the victims, was brought in as the next witness. Her father sat in the gallery as the tearful, attractive widow testified. She stated that she and Ray had been married since 1921 and had no children. She stated she and her husband had gone out to the movies on the night he was killed. They had arrived home at 10:45 p.m., at which time he got ready for work, and she packed his lunch. He left for work about fifteen minutes later. She went on to say that he was a second helper on the open hearth. Through uncontrollable sobs, she managed to state that less than an hour after he had left the house, she got the report that he was dead. The defense did not cross-examine her, as it would not have benefited their case if they had done so. Rock was an experienced attorney—he knew better. Mrs. Kochendarfer was excused from the stand but remained in the courtroom. She sat with her father and Anna Messer in the front row of the gallery.

Wheeling Steel employment manager Wade Bougher was the next to testify about Dasco's employment at the mill. He stated that Dasco began his employment at the mill on October 25, 1929. He worked as a laborer in the construction department. In September 1933, he was transferred to the new process department. Attorney Thomas Rock asked to see the employment card, and Bougher showed it to him, saying that Dasco's personal disposition was good (meaning he got along with other employees).

The paymaster, Ray Fisher, was next to testify regarding Dasco's timecards from January 31 to July 1934. He stated that Dasco had punched in on March 3 at 2:45 p.m. and out at 11:05 p.m. On May 30, he punched in at 2:44 p.m. and out at 11:01 p.m. After objecting to the paymaster's testimony as irrelevant, Tom Rock was overruled. When asked by the state if Dasco worked on the night of July 1, Fisher stated that the records did not show he did. Rock did not cross-examine Fisher, and he was excused. The timecards were entered into evidence despite an objection from the defense.

Ward Artman, a Wheeling Steel police officer, took the stand. He stated that he worked the night of July 1 and punched out at 2:20 a.m. on July 2. He testified that Harold Morken, who he'd known for twenty years, came into the clock office on March 5 and said that Morken stated he was looking for a man. At that point, Rock objected by shouting, "Hearsay!" His objection was sustained after the prosecutor and defense attorneys were asked to approach the bench. After conferring with the judge, the prosecutor was forced to change his approach. Hooper asked Artman if he saw Dasco on the night of July 1. Artman stated, "Yes, I did. He came in around 10:20 p.m. I stayed at the gate until 12: 30 a.m. but didn't see Dasco again." Gavin cross-examined Artman, hammering at his testimony, but it didn't shake him. "Isn't it true that a man could leave by the mill gate and not be identified?" Artman replied, "No one passed by me on July 1 without being observed."

Prosecutor Hooper called one of his chief witnesses, Harold "Babe" Morken, the man who first identified David Dasco as the mill shooter. Morken stated that, on the night of March 3, he saw Dasco near the mill cafeteria with a gun in his hand. He reported the sighting to Chief McCloskey, who had Morken point Dasco out to him on March 5. Chief William McCloskey stated, under oath, that it wasn't until July 5 that he ordered Lieutenants Major and McGough to trail Dasco. Thomas Rock cross-examined McCloskey. "You didn't do anything until July 5, even after you were made aware of a man carrying a gun?" McCloskey replied, "No." Rock shook his head. "No more questions for this witness."

During the trial, two eyewitnesses to the double shooting at the mill were identified: James Porter and Mel Looman. James Porter was called to the stand on the fourth day of the trial; he was the second witness to take the stand that morning. "I knew both Ray Kochendarfer and William Messer," Porter stated when asked by Prosecutor Hooper whether he knew the victims. When asked, James Porter told the court that he worked in the open hearth with the two victims and saw the shooting the night of July 1. "Dasco is the man that I saw shoot Ray Kochendarfer," he stated. James Porter explained that he had met up with Kochendarfer at 11:20 p.m. in the cafeteria, where they spent a few minutes talking. "I was about thirty-five feet behind Kochendarfer and Messer when I heard two shots ring out. There was a pause; then, I heard three more shots. I watched both men fall in front of me." Porter bowed his head at the memory.

Prosecutor Hooper asked Porter to continue. "The guy ran between the two bodies and the steps of the open hearth. He crossed the railroad tracks, toward the Ohio River, then ran along the tracks toward Mingo." Porter went on, "He wore a black mill cap, large black coat and huge black trousers. When he ran, he wobbled like an old man, waving a gun around in his hand. Dasco is the man I saw shoot Ray Kochendarfer," James Porter declared. On cross-examination, Rock managed to get Porter to admit that he didn't see Dasco's face. Porter stated that he knew it was Dasco when he saw him at the county jail. "I recognized his clothes, and when they made him run, I recognized his ape-like gait. It's him," Porter stated flatly.

Mel Looman, the other eyewitness to the double shooting, was also an open-hearth employee and had worked at Wheeling Steel for thirty-two years. He testified to hearing the shots. "I stepped out of the shanty, under the stairs leading to the open hearth. I saw a man run by me with a gun in his hand. He had passed within ten to fifteen feet of me, waving the gun in my direction. That's when I saw the right side of his face as he made his way toward the river with a peculiar, slow gait."

Thomas Rock began his cross-examination by asking Looman, "So what did the right side of the man's face look like?" The reply from Looman was, "He either had a dirty face or a heavy beard." Rock shouted, "You don't know what it was, do you?" Looman replied, "No." He admitted that he had identified Dasco when he saw his face and watched him walk and run at the county jail. Rock advised that he had no more questions for this witness.

Millworker Jay Davis stated that he had observed on three separate occasions, from January to June, a man peering into the cafeteria window. "One time," Davis said, "I even caught him sitting in my car. Another time, outside the cafeteria, he was standing on my fender. I asked him what he thought he was doing. The guy replied, 'Me want nothing, just looking for man in cafeteria.' I looked right at him that time. It was David Dasco." Davis continued, "When the two killings happened in July, I saw Dasco enter the cafeteria, and I realized that he fit the description of the man police were looking for. I went and reported it to the mill police, but they refused to arrest Dasco at the time." Gavin and Rock objected to much of Davis's testimony, saying it was irrelevant, but the testimony remained on the record.

John Japczynski, who lived in a bungalow behind the Popovich house, where Dasco roomed, testified that, on July 1, the day of the double shooting, he watched from his window as Dasco came out of the Popovich home and walked toward Beatty Park. Japczynski said, "He ritualistically walked back and forth between the Popovich home and the park at least fifteen times, which took about two hours to complete." Japczynski stated that Dasco was wearing a black, shiny peaked hat, dark trousers, shoes and a soiled blue shirt while carrying a dark jacket. As his testimony continued, Japczynski said he didn't become suspicious of his neighbor until he read the newspaper the next day and read about the double murder at the mill. Prosecutor Hooper inquired of Japczynski, "Have you ever seen David Dasco wear a suit, such as he's wearing today?" The witness replied, "No, never." The audience laughed at the answer, causing Clerk Cavanaugh to give them a warning to be quiet. "Mr. Japczynski," Gavin began with his cross-examination, "you kept track of Mr. Dasco pretty well, didn't you?" Japczynski replied, "No, I was merely observing the fact that he was coming in and out of the house so many times. Like I said, I didn't become suspicious of him until the next day." Gavin had no further questions for the witness.

Lieutenant C.H. Bailey and Officer John P. Fonow, who had followed and arrested David Dasco on the night of July 28, gave their testimony. George Jester, a millworker in the annealing department of the new process area, where Dasco was a sweeper, aided them in the arrest. He, too, was called to the witness stand. Lieutenant Bailey, a mill police officer, described the night of July 28, when he took up the twenty-minute, circuitous trail of the defendant through the mill. He described how Dasco had entered the old sheet mill annealing plant through a hole in the building and climbed, over several piles of steel sheets, to the west side of the room. He walked south, to the west side of the old electrical shop. During that part of the mysterious hike through the mill, Bailey enlisted the aid of George Jester to trail Dasco. The men continued to follow Dasco, who had realized he was being followed as he made his way toward the gate, where Officer Fonow stopped him.

Bailey continued to tell his story about the finding of the revolver, the homemade holster and six extra shells on Dasco. Hooper showed him the Colt .38 revolver, which was entered into evidence after Bailey identified it as the gun that he had taken from Dasco. Bailey continued to say that they took Dasco to the main gate and summoned the Steubenville police. Bailey said Officers Sam Baker and Earl Long arrived within a few minutes and took Dasco to the city jail. Fonow, Bailey and Jester followed, and Bailey said he had turned the revolver over to Captain Frank Taylor at the city jail.

Under cross-examination by Tom Rock, Bailey stated that he had been employed as a guard during a strike in 1927 at the Pittsburgh Terminal Coal Company. "Are you particularly interested in this case?" Rock inquired. Bailey's reply was, "Yes, ever since Fred Melsheimer was shot." Rock questioned, "Are you interested in the reward?" Bailey replied, "Yes, but duty comes first." Rock retorted, "Haven't you made overtures to a certain woman to leave town with you once you get the reward or part of it?"

"No!" Bailey replied.

"Do you know a woman named Daisy?" Rock kept pushing.

"Yes."

Pushing a little more, Rock questioned, "She lives with you—isn't that correct?"

"No, I room at her place," answered Bailey. After a few more questions from Rock, Bailey was excused.

Then, George Jester was called—just long enough to corroborate Bailey's testimony.

John P. Fonow, the mill officer who assisted in Dasco's arrest, stated that, on several occasions after July 23, he had observed that, when workers clocked out, he noticed Dasco standing outside the regular line. Tom Rock objected to Fonow's testimony but was overruled.

Lloyd B. Trunk, an assistant ballistics expert from Cleveland, paved the way to David Cowles's testimony by merely stating that he had received the revolver and some bullets in July from Patrolman Robert Doyle. He identified the revolver as the one given to him by Doyle. This established a chain of evidence regarding the weapon. David Cowles, a renowned Cleveland ballistics expert, testified about the bullets taken from each man. "The bullets taken from each man matched with bullets fired from the gun taken from David Dasco." Rock tried to dispute his testimony, but Cowles came prepared with photographs of the microscopic comparisons of those bullets with the bullets fired from Lieutenant Marshall Jack's gun. After Cowles made his point, Rock backed off.

Steubenville police officer Sam Baker, who had transported Dasco to the jail on July 28, identified the overalls with a canvas holster attached inside the leg as the ones that had been taken from the defendant that night. He also identified a black sleeve as belonging to Dasco; inside the sleeve was a black leather holster. The wrapped holster had been discovered in Dasco's back pocket. A black cap and overcoat were shown to Baker, and he identified those as belonging to the defendants too. All of the items were admitted into evidence over Rock's objections.

Baker then said that he went to the Popovich residence at 634½ Lincoln Avenue later that evening to perform a search of Dasco's room for evidence. He stated that Chief Ross Cunningham and Patrolman David Lyle accompanied him. In a bottom dresser drawer, Baker said he found a file under a pile of clothes that contained articles about the mill shootings from the *Steubenville Herald Star* and the Wheeling and Pittsburgh papers. Gavin and Rock raised numerous objections to Patrolman Baker's testimony but were overruled. Gavin said he couldn't possibly see how newspapers could be ruled into evidence. Judge Oglevee withheld his ruling, stating he would like to look through the papers first. He granted the defense attorneys the right to recall Officer Baker for cross-examination after his ruling. The judge was then seen perusing the newspapers, which were allowed into evidence. Gavin cross-examined Baker for a few more minutes.

Then Sheriff Ray B. Long took the stand. He identified a couple of the bullets that he had found near the bodies of Kochendarfer and Messer. Long stated that Dasco had told him about making the holster that was found buttoned inside his pants. He told the courtroom Dasco's story of purchasing the gun a few days before his arrest from some man for seventy-five cents. The sheriff was asked by Rock during cross-examination whether he remembered Dasco saying the phrase, "If I talk, I die; if I don't talk, I live."

"Yes," Sheriff Long answered, "he said it a few times."

Rock prodded, "Do you think he was serious when he said it?"

"He was in jail, wasn't he?" the sheriff shot back. "He didn't appear to be joking," he added quickly.

Rock continued his grilling of Sheriff Long. "Sheriff, during all of your conversations with my client, did he always maintain his innocence and tell the same stories?"

"Yes, practically," the sheriff replied.

"Has he been a model prisoner?"

"Yes, he has," answered the sheriff. He was then excused from the stand.

The star witness, J.W. Johnson, one of the mill's crane operators, testified to seeing Dasco flee from the scene of the double shootings on July 1. Dasco had passed within fifteen feet of Johnson, and under ridgid cross-examination by the experienced Tom Rock, Johnson remained unshaken in his testimony. The state rested its case against David Dasco.

20

THE PHANTOM TESTIFIES

In a bold move that rarely happens in a murder trial, David Dasco took the witness stand. Speaking in a clear voice, with only a hint of an accent, Dasco proclaimed his innocence in all the shootings at Wheeling Steel. Dasco answered every question that his attorneys threw at him. After they were done, Prosecutor Hooper and his assistant, Harry Chalfant, put the defendant through a brutal cross-examination. He withstood their questioning.

The sly Tom Rock had Dasco demonstrate his running skills to the jury by having him run across the courtroom. The forty-eight-year-old Dasco made the run for his life by starting in front of the jury box. With his head up and knees high, he ran across the courtroom, stopping himself against the far wall. The stunt was well-planned and well-played, as Dasco ran fast, considering his age and his double hernia. The crowd of spectators in the courtroom seemed to love it.

Tom Rock asked the defendant about his life and his movements after coming to the United States. Dasco told the jurors and curious spectators that he had been born in Roccacasale, Italy. His father died about six years earlier. He didn't know if his mother was still alive or not. He had two brothers in Italy and no family in America. He came to America in 1909 and arrived at Ellis Island in New York. He went to Pittsburgh from there and then to Youngstown, where he worked as a laborer for three years. After that, he went back to Pittsburgh. Dasco served in the World War after he was drafted in June 1918. Forty-five days later, he was shipped to France, where he participated in the Meuse-Argonne offensive. He received a flesh wound during the battle, and his honorable discharge was accepted into evidence. Upon his discharge, he returned to Pittsburgh, where he stayed for a while before going to work in Ambridge, Pennsylvania. From Ambridge, he moved to Steubenville in 1929.

Under direct examination from his attorney, Dasco answered a barrage of questions. "Dave, after your arrest and being taken to the police station, do you remember who questioned you?"

"Yes," Dasco replied. "It was Chief Cunningham, Mr. Schroeder and some other men."

"Did they ask you about the killings?" Rock continued.

"Yes, I told them I knew nothing about them."

Rock pressed on. "Dave, did they question you until the morning of the next day?"

Dasco answered, "Yes, they did. They questioned me for hours. Prosecutor Hooper was there, too."

"Dave," Rock queried, "where did you get the gun that was found on you the night you were arrested?"

The defendant replied, "I bought it near the Ohio Pottery Company on North High Street when I walked up there to get a drink from the spring. Lots of people go there for water. Some guy came up to me and asked if I wanted to buy it."

Rock asked who this man was. Dasco stated that he didn't know the guy. "He was about forty years old, was a little shorter than me and was clean-shaven. He wore clothes like a millworker." Dasco continued, "I saw him near the pottery. He asked me if I wanted to buy a gun. I said no. He said he'd sell it for seventy-five cents. I said okay. He gave me the gun, the leather holster and eighteen bullets. This was four days before I got arrested. I never fired the gun."

The gun was shown to Dasco. He said he couldn't tell if it was his for sure because he only had it for a short time. When asked if he had ever been arrested before, Dasco replied, "Yes, I was arrested once for disorderly conduct and spent a night in jail. That was one year before I came to Steubenville. I haven't been in any trouble since then." Dasco was then shown a set of blueprints of the Wheeling Steel Plant in Steubenville. Upon request of his attorney, Thomas Rock, he was asked to trace the route he took after he clocked out the night he was arrested. The little Italian said that he walked over to the cafeteria to get some cookies and then returned to the new process building, where he worked, to get the gloves he left on a barrel there.

Rock reminded his client that the state claimed, per Bailey's testimony, that he'd taken a long, circuitous route through the mill. Dasco testified that he had not—that he'd gone straight back to the new process building. "I found my gloves, but when they arrested me, they took the gloves out of my pocket and didn't give them back," Dasco explained, refuting the state's witness testimony. Rock continued questioning his client. "Dave, why did you buy the gun? Wasn't it after the killings and some robberies that had happened at work?" Dasco stated that the robberies were the reason he had purchased the gun, which came with eighteen loaded shells. He claimed he had never fired the gun or cleaned it.

Prodded by Rock, Dasco said that, as a sweeper in the new process department, his boss would often send him to the cafeteria to pick up food for the workers there. He said that he would make five or six trips to the cafeteria during his shift. Rock asked, "David, did you ever say, in the presence of Sheriff Long and Prosecutor Hooper and a *Herald Star* reporter, 'If I talk, I die; if I don't talk, I'll live'?" Dasco denied ever saying the phrase, with an emphatic, "No."

Prosecutor Hooper began his cross-examination of the accused man, covering all the inconsistencies in Dasco's testimony. "Didn't you say that you made this holster in front of the *Herald Star* reporter?" Hooper pointed to the black leather holster in evidence. "No, I never said I made it to anyone," Dasco said. When asked why he carried the six extra bullets that had been found on him the night of the arrest, Dasco replied, "I was going to go out in the country and try out the revolver."

Hooper prodded, "Don't you know that one of the shells you had was an empty one?"

"No, they were all loaded. There were no empty shells," insisted Dasco.

"Isn't it true that you only needed five bullets to reload after you used five bullets to shoot Kochendarfer and Messer?"

"No, no," Dasco replied. Defense attorney Rock leaped to his feet, objecting to the prosecutor's tactics. Judge Oglevee overruled the objection.

"You carried that gun with you to work and hid it in the mill every night." Hooper was striking a nerve with each question he fired at Dasco.

Dasco answered, "No, I did not."

"You worked all evening with the gun strapped to your leg?"

"Yes, I did," Dasco insisted.

Prosecutor Hooper went on the attack, challenging the route through the mill that Dasco took on the night of his arrest. Lieutenant Bailey contended that he had followed Dasco on a circuitous route that ended at the gate.

Dasco's story that he had just gone to the cafeteria then back to his worksite was a totally different account of that night. The accused man did not waver from that account. As Hooper introduced the crude, hand-sewn mask that was found in Dasco's room the night he was arrested into evidence, he handed it to the man. Smiling, Dasco put it on his face, admitting that he'd made it for himself. He denied having a second mask when Hooper asked him.

Tom Rock put his own ballistics expert on the stand, but the expert confirmed the findings of David Cowles. Rock had attempted to show that ballistics was not an exact science. After a short recess, the other defense witnesses were sworn in to take the stand—the first one being Ralph Carmichael. Carmichael worked with Kochendarfer and Messer and knew them quite well. He confirmed for Rock that neither of the victims knew Fred Melsheimer or James Barnett, the other victims. Rock was trying to show that there was no connection between the shootings of the first two victims and the last two.

Elba Johnson, another witness for the defense, was a crane operator near the open-hearth department. He was standing next to Mel Looman and George Schroeder, who claimed they recognized Dasco as he ran by them after the double shooting. Elba Johnson claimed he couldn't recognize the shooter. He also claimed that the shooter waved the gun but didn't point it at anyone. Rock had Dasco stand up and ask Johnson, "Do you recognize this man as the shooter?" Johnson said, "No, I couldn't see the shooter, and I was standing beside Looman and Schroeder." When he was asked the same question by the prosecutor, Johnson remained steadfast on his answer.

Mrs. Margaret Bonzer, a resident of 408 Washington Street, was next to be called by the defense. She responded to Rock's questions, stating that David Dasco lived in a rooming house she owned on South Third Street in 1932, having roomed there for a month. She went on to say that she had purchased a rooming house on South Fifth Street and that Dasco had moved into that rooming house. Rock pressed on, "Mrs. Bonzer, did you ever notice newspaper clippings in Dasco's room?"

"Oh, yes, David always had newspaper clippings lying around. I used to see them all the time," said Margaret Bonzer.

Rock continued, "Mrs. Bonzer, did you find a clipping of President Coolidge's funeral in his room?"

"Yes, he had a clipping of the eulogy given for President Calvin Coolidge that he saved. I have it with me," she offered, handing it to Tom Rock.

Rock attempted to put the eulogy into evidence, hoping it would show the patriotic, human side of his client; Prosecutor Hooper objected furiously but was overruled. Under cross-examination, Prosecutor Hooper asked Mrs. Bonzer, "How is it that you have a clipping in your possession that belonged to the defendant?"

"It was among a bunch of other clippings that David left in a dresser drawer when he moved out. I just saved them," she replied. "He was a very good tenant and always paid his rent," she added, when asked by defense attorney Rock.

Ben Hart, who worked side-by-side with Dasco as a sweeper in the new process department, stated that he often went with Dasco to the cafeteria to get food for the other workmen. He testified that he never saw Dasco with a gun at work in the year that he worked with the man. Prosecutor Hooper asked Hart, "Isn't it a fact that Mr. Dasco was wearing that gun on his person while working on the night of July 28?" Hart answered, "No, not then—not ever."

"Did you walk out to the time clock with Dasco sometimes?"

"Yes, we walked out together all the time," Hart replied. In answer to the prosecutor's next question, he answered, "No, I never saw Dasco stand out of line at the time clock. He never did that."

Mrs. Susan Popovich, who was the defendant's last landlady, took the stand for the defense. "I've known David for two years, since he came to room at our home on August 16, 1932." When prodded by Tom Rock, she stated, "He had blinds on his window but only a rag over the doorknob." This last remark was to dispute the state's claim that the keyhole had been plugged. She said he had put papers up on the French door that faced the street because there was no blind. "He was a good, quiet tenant the entire two years that he lived with me and my husband." Mrs. Popovich stepped down from the stand. Her husband, Andrew, was supposed to testify to the same things, but he spoke little English. No interpreter was available, so he was dismissed.

Mike Scarponi testified that he had known David Dasco for the last five years. They roomed together from 1929 to 1930 and even slept in the same bed. He described Dasco as a quiet, peaceable man. Scarponi delivered his short testimony then stepped down. Thomas Rock and P.A. Gavin rested their case in the fight to save the life of David Dasco, the alleged Phantom Killer of the Wheeling Steel Yard of Steubenville, Ohio.

Gavin began his final argument, saying, "Can the state argue that a man can, in a twinkling of an eye, step from the path of honesty and become a foul criminal? It is impossible for this man, with the excellent background he has, to suddenly become a midnight assassin, skulking in the darkness." Gavin continued his riveting speech: "There has not been a scintilla of evidence presented in this court that would point the finger of suspicion at this defendant, until late in July, until rewards totaling $6,000 were offered for the capture and conviction of the killer." Gavin continued his spellbinding speech: "Not until then did all kinds of hawkshaws appear, all united in pointing their fingers at someone. If this defendant is to go to the electric chair, there must be no doubt as to his guilt." He ended his final argument by calling David Cowles's testimony "ballistics monkeyshines." Gavin then asked for acquittal, saying they had proven cause.

Prosecutor Hooper started his final argument by going over his witnesses' testimonies and showing the display of evidence. At the end of his argument, Hooper held up a large photograph of Ray Kochendarfer, the handsome young husband who had been gunned down. The crowd, and especially the jurors, were riveted by seeing the man they had been discussing throughout the trial. "The man who ran away from the spot where Ray Kochendarfer was killed—that man was David Dasco," Hooper bellowed, pointing an accusatory finger at the defendant. "He took his life without any reason, without any provocation, just as you would shoot a dog in the street." Prosecutor Hooper went on, saying, "I say to you, ladies and gentlemen, there has never been a more cold-blooded case in this county than that of Ray Kochendarfer by this defendant. All I ask from the jury is that you assume your responsibilities squarely. I am confident that you will reach but one conclusion—that conclusion being guilty as charged, without the recommendation of mercy." Dorothy Kochendarfer, who was sitting in the gallery, sobbed at the sight of her husband's face. William Messer's widow, Anna, who was sitting beside her, rested a comforting hand on her arm.

Judge Oglevee read the four possible verdicts to the jury. First-degree murder without mercy meant the death penalty; Dasco would die in the electric chair. First-degree murder with mercy meant a life sentence in the Ohio Penitentiary. Second-degree murder meant life in the penitentiary with the possibility of a pardon. A not-guilty verdict would free Dasco of the charge of killing Ray Kochendarfer.

When Judge Oglevee finished his instructions, William Fellows, the jurors' assigned court bailiff, led them to the Fort Steuben Hotel, where they spent their time determining a man's fate. The thirteenth juror, Matt Friend, was dismissed from his duties after the jury took their leave. The Phantom Killer headlines were drawing to a close with the decision of twelve ordinary people.

21

THE VERDICT

On Saturday, October 28, the sensational Phantom Killer murder trial came to an end. At 4:21 p.m., the case was turned over to the jury of five women and seven men. Arthur Hooper's worry that the women would be too merciful, swaying the others to acquit or creating a hung jury, was weighing on his prosecutorial mind. Defense attorneys Thomas Rock and P.A. Gavin, on the other hand, were counting on it. The jury was deliberating only on the Ray Kochendarfer murder charge. The two other murder charges, in the cases of William Messer and Fred Melsheimer, were still pending. Should Dasco be acquitted, one of those cases would be used to try him again. Not to be forgotten was the attempted murder charge concerning James Barnett. Barnett, who was the only survivor of the phantom gunman, had been crippled by one of the bullets. Originally paralyzed by Dasco, it was thought that he would never walk again, but he was able to walk with crutches, due to his amazing resilience and perseverance.

As David D'Ascanio awaited his fate, the guys he competed with in the newspaper headlines were getting their comeuppance as well. Adam Richetti, the right-hand man of the now deceased Pretty Boy Floyd, was fighting extradition back to Kansas City, Missouri, where he faced his own murder trial. John Dillinger, who had been killed six days before Dasco was arrested, had caused a big blow-up in Crown Point, Indiana, as it had been discovered that many people had been involved in helping Dillinger escape. The roundup of all the culprits had started as Lake County, Indiana sheriff

Lillian Holley seethed. The headlines were still jumping with news as the Phantom Killer's front-page time was coming to an end.

On Saturday evening, the jurors discussed the case in their quarters at the Fort Steuben Hotel. Their first ballot was ten to two in favor of a guilty without mercy verdict. They asked their bailiff, William Fellows, to ask Judge Oglevee if a recommendation of life with mercy would mean that David Dasco could be pardoned later. The answer came back from the judge—no, he could not be pardoned later. After they learned Dasco couldn't be pardoned, they took another vote. That vote came back eleven to one in favor of life with mercy. The two original holdouts were satisfied of Dasco's guilt but had some lingering doubts. They continued deliberating until midnight, when Judge Oglevee summoned them back to the courthouse. A crowd of people was still there after waiting all night for the verdict.

Sheriff Ray Long went to Dasco's cell. "Get ready, Dasco, we need to be at the courthouse in ten minutes," the sheriff ordered.

"I can't be ready in ten minutes," was the gruff reply from the prisoner.

Long opened the cell door and put the cuffs on him. "Let's go."

When they arrived at the courthouse, just before midnight, Long led the disgruntled little man to his chair. His two attorneys were already seated at their table. The flash of anger shone in Dasco's eyes as he mumbled and grunted. Thomas Rock told him to be quiet, but Dasco continued to visibly show his extreme irritation. "They tell me everything I gotta do," he raged. A very irritated Rock turned to Dasco. "I said be quiet," he admonished his client.

The jurors, one by one, took their places in the jury box as Judge Oglevee took the bench. Alonzo McCue, the jury foreman, informed the judge that they hadn't come to an agreement yet. They were dismissed until 9:00 a.m. Monday morning. Everybody filed out of the courthouse, and a mumbling Dasco was taken back to his cell.

At 9:00 a.m., the crowd, attorneys and Dasco were all seated as the jury came in. As soon as Judge Oglevee took the bench, jury foreman McCue handed him a written note, asking him to read the law on the charge of murder, which the judge did. He dismissed the jury at 9:15 a.m.; at that time, they returned to the Fort Steuben Hotel in the company of their bailiff.

Court was called into session at 12:08 p.m., after the judge was notified that a verdict had been reached. The jury delivered its verdict before the waiting crowd, the attorneys and David Dasco. Alonzo McCue stood and handed the verdict to clerk Kenneth Cavanaugh, who, in turn, handed it to Judge Oglevee. Oglevee handed it back, instructing Cavanaugh to read it.

Bailiff William Fellows warned the crowded gallery that there would be no trouble after the verdict was read. In a clear voice, Cavanaugh read the long-awaited fate of David Dasco: "On the charge of murder in the first degree, the jury finds the defendant, David Dasco, guilty, with a recommendation of life with mercy."

David Dasco sat in the courtroom, showing little emotion. The crowd was disappointed when Judge Oglevee recessed court until 1:30 p.m. He advised that he would not pass a sentence until the defense attorneys filed their motion for a new trial. The defense attorneys would have three days to file the motion. "They do nothing to me," Dasco was overheard saying. He was speaking to a friend he had worked with years ago who had come to visit him at the jail. "I will be free soon," he boasted, thinking he would soon be granted a new trial. The two murder charges that had been shelved for that purpose had not crossed his mind. "I will be out in a few days," he told deputies.

"The motion for a new trial is overruled," Judge Oglevee announced on Friday, November 2, to defense attorneys Rock and Gavin. As expected, the judge sentenced David Dasco to life in prison without the possibility of pardon. He asked Sheriff Long to take the condemned man to the Ohio Penitentiary without delay. The judge continued, "Do you have anything you wish to say, Mr. Dasco?"

"I have nothing to say," Dasco replied, the sound of defeat in his voice. Deputies overhead Dasco mumbling in his cell, later in the day, "I'll get out sometime. I must get out; this is no place for me."

On Thursday, November 8, Sheriff Ray B. Long shackled the Phantom, David Dasco, for the last time in the Jefferson County Jail at his cell on the second tier. Juvenile officer William Campbell assisted the sheriff in getting Dasco ready. "You have anything to say, Dave?" Campbell asked.

"Yes," Dasco replied, "I didn't do it, I didn't do it." Handing Campbell the outfit he had worn in court, Dasco said, "Give these to my attorneys. I may need them again for court."

Accompanied by Deputy Charles Merryman, Sheriff Long escorted Dasco to the squad car. They made the long drive to the Ohio Penitentiary in Columbus, where the Phantom was handed over to prison authorities later that afternoon. On December 17, the fifth district court of appeals postponed the appeal until June 1935.

22

REWARD CLAIMS POUR IN

On January 9, 1935, Harold Morken, the millworker who was the first to report Dasco as the mill killer on March 3, after seeing Dasco outside the mill cafeteria with a revolver in his hand, put in a claim for the Wheeling Steel Corporation's reward. He reported what he saw to mill police, who did nothing. He saw Dasco again on March 5 and July 23 and reported it to mill police, who still did nothing.

Morken hired Steubenville attorney Stuart Moreland to act on his behalf. It was Moreland who wrote letters to the Jefferson County commissioners and Wheeling Steel officials asking for the full amount of the reward, since Morken gave testimony to the grand jury and testified in the trial that ended in the conviction of David Dasco.

On February 15, Morken, then a former employee of Wheeling Steel, prepared to file suit to get the reward. Prosecutor Hooper and Wheeling Steel management advised him to hold off until David Dasco's appeal was heard in the court of appeals. Prosecutor Hooper told Morken that he was not the only one who would try to claim the reward and that they needed to hold off until those claims started coming in. After the appeal was heard, a list of people entitled to the reward would come forward. John P. Fonow, C.H. Bailey, John Japczynski, James Porter and Jay Davis were the next to make claims on the reward.

On June 3, 1935, Prosecutor Hooper was successful, once again, in his verbal battle with Dasco's defense attorneys, Gavin and Rock, in their appeal to get their client freed from his life sentence. The appeal was denied, and Dasco remained in prison.

Wheeling Steel corporation president W.W. Holloway, deluged by attorney letters, put out an announcement that appeared in the *Steubenville Herald Star* on July 23. It read:

> *David D'Ascanio, alias Dasco, has been convicted of the murder of Ray Kochendarfer. The reward will be paid if and when the conviction is affirmed by the highest court to which it is appealed.*
>
> *In order that the undersigned may determine the person or persons and the amount of the award to which each is entitled, every person desiring consideration of this claim for all or any portion of the reward, is requested to submit to the undersigned, by mail, on or before the 24th of August, 1935, his name and address, and his statement of activities in connection with the case which should be considered in the distribution of the reward.*
>
> *Signed, W.W. Holloway, president, Wheeling Steel Corporation*

Victor Galownia, who had seen Dasco lay his gun on a sink in the mill washroom and informed the prosecutor, put in a claim for the reward, too. There was no written record of his sighting.

On December 18, W.W. Holloway announced that he had made his list of persons entitled to the $5,000 reward offered by Wheeling Steel for the arrest and conviction of the Phantom Killer. The next day, the list was announced in the *Herald Star*.

Harold Morken received $1,250, the largest portion of the $5,000; Lieutenant Clarence H. Bailey, who tailed and arrested Dasco, received $900; John Fonow, a mill police officer, received $350; John Japczynski, Melvin Looman, Walter Schroeder, M.J. Major, James Porter and J.W. Johnson received $250; Thomas Dignan, Ernest Schroeder and R.V. McGough received $200; and D.G. Campbell, George Artman, J.L. Davis and George Jester each got $100. It remained to be seen who was entitled to the $1,000 reward that the Jefferson County commissioners had offered.

At the end of December 1935, Sheriff Long escorted a prisoner to the Ohio Penitentiary. While there, he was informed that David Dasco was not doing well. Dasco's guards informed the sheriff that the convicted killer had been ill for some time and could no longer perform his duties as a sweeper in the prison. The dementia that he had been diagnosed with after his arrest seemed to have taken control of his mind and body. He no longer responded to greetings by other prisoners, he quit talking and his mind appeared to be gone. Guards had relieved him of his sweeper duties, and they surmised that the Phantom Killer didn't have long to live. Sheriff Long thanked them for the report.

It wasn't until the beginning of 1936 that Jefferson County commissioners released a list of eleven persons who would share in the $1,000 reward. Harold Morken received $300.29; Lieutenant C.H. Bailey received $224.80; David G. Campbell got $29.20; Jay L. Davis got $20.60; John P. Fonow got $81.50; John Japczynski got $66.20; J.W. Johnson got $66.20; James Porter got $66.20; Walter W. Schroeder got $66.20; Otto Shelton got $29.60; and Victor Galownia got $29.60. Dispersing the reward money brought that chapter of the case to a close.

In February 1936, a claim of newly found evidence in the Dasco case caused his defense attorneys, Thomas Rock and Peter A. Gavin, to file a petition asking that the bill of exceptions in the case of the State of Ohio against David Dasco and the evidence in the case be impounded together with all exhibits. This action would assure the safety of all records pertaining to the case if a motion were to be filed for a new trial. Common pleas court judge Frank F. Cope granted the petition. Clerk Frank Mapel took custody of the bill of exceptions, evidence and exhibits. The day for another trial never happened.

David Dasco, whose real name was Davidio D'Ascanio, was a quiet loner who worked out and kept to himself. He enjoyed the solitude of sitting on the wall at Beatty Park. Dasco served in World War I in the infantry and was in the trenches in France during the Meuse-Argonne offensive. He was even listed as missing in action for a few weeks (this is probably when he was wounded). He earned his American citizenship after serving and giving his allegiance to the United States. He was convicted of the phantom killings at Wheeling Steel and was sent to the Ohio Penitentiary for his murderous crimes. Some people still thought, at that time, that he had been framed as the frenzy to collect the reward grew.

His health declined soon after he arrived at the prison, where he had become a sweeper. As dementia took its hold on his mind and body, prison officials had him transferred to Lima State Hospital for the Criminally Insane in Lima, Ohio. The once-stocky and strong Dasco had become a thin wisp of himself. He remained there until he died on February 1, 1947. His body was shipped back to the Mosti Funeral Home in Steubenville, Ohio, where Mrs. Louis Sellaroli of Steubenville, a family friend of D'Ascanio's late parents in Italy, claimed the body. Mary Sellaroli took care of all the expenses for his funeral, which was held at St. Anthony's Church in Steubenville. His pallbearers were Michael Scarponi, Angelo DiPietre,

David D'Ascanio "Dasco's" unmarked gravesite at Mount Calvary Cemetery. *From the collection of Susan Guy.*

Carol Ratondo, Luigi Gentele, Dominic Grossi and Cesta Massenino. He was laid to rest at Mount Calvary Cemetery in an unmarked grave. No motive was ever determined for the crimes. Was it possible that he suffered from shellshock (as it was called at the time) from the effects of war? Did Hitler's advancement of Nazism throughout Europe lead to his mental breakdown, worrying over his brothers' safety in Italy? What had actually happened to David D'Ascanio in the days that he was missing in action during World War I? We will never know.

23

THOSE LEFT BEHIND

A nna Messer, the widow of Dasco's murder victim William Messer, was left with four children to raise. The oldest two sons, Charles (nineteen) and James (seventeen), worked to help their mother. The two girls were a little younger. Wheeling Steel Corporation never compensated any of the victims' families for the deaths of their loved ones. Messer was the only victim to have children left behind to mourn his loss.

In 1939, almost five years after her husband's death, Anna filed suit in common pleas court against the industrial commission of Ohio. The final ruling of the industrial commission held that she was not entitled to death benefits, on the grounds that her husband didn't meet his death as a result of injury sustained in the regular course of his employment with the Wheeling Steel Corporation.

Anna's oldest son, Charles, became a drunk after his father was murdered. He was picked up by Steubenville police for a couple of menial crimes. He died at the age of twenty-one during an operation to remove a brain tumor. Her other son, James, died at the age of forty-one. He allegedly asphyxiated on food that he had regurgitated and was found lying in the doorway of his bedroom. His son left a note telling his mother that he had gone on to school. James's wife was in Wheeling, visiting a relative overnight. When she came home the next morning, she found her husband covered with a blanket and the note pinned to it. She called the police, who interviewed their son, Butch. He said his father and three men were drinking and arguing in the kitchen. He saw one of the men drag his dad to the bedroom doorway at

7:30 a.m. When the guy saw Butch, he mumbled, "I gotta go for help," and ran out the door. Anna outlived all of her children, except for one daughter, Leah. Anna died in 1963.

James Barnett, the second victim of the Phantom and the only one to survive, was maimed by two bullets. One of the bullets lodged in his hip and paralyzed him; doctors thought that he would never walk again, but by some miracle, he recovered enough to walk with crutches and, then, a cane. One leg remained paralyzed. In 1940, he fell backward down a flight of stairs at the Jefferson County Courthouse; this led to severe bodily injuries. He was escorted to his residence at 705 North Court by a deputy. He sued the county commissioners for $5,000, stating his fall was due to a loose handrail on the courthouse stairs. He won his case.

Around 1942, Barnett moved to Cleveland for a short time before moving to Highspire, Dauphin County, Pennsylvania, in October 1942. He worked at the Middletown Air Depot and lived in a dormitory on the site. On December 29, 1943, at 2:00 a.m., James Joseph Barnett, at the age of fifty-three, was found on the floor next to his bed by a fellow employee—he was dead. The cause of his death was listed as acute fatal gastric hemorrhage, and its origin was unknown.

John Paul Fonow, the mill police officer who captured the Phantom Killer, David Dasco, had an interest in law enforcement before being sworn in as an officer at Wheeling Steel. His brother, Frank Fonow, was a Steubenville police officer. During the 1932 elections, he ran for sheriff against Ray B. Long and Archie Bell, who later became the Jefferson County coroner. He became a crane operator at Wheeling Steel and served as a Toronto city councilman for many years. He died in 1966 at the age of seventy-one.

Lieutenant Clarence Harvey Bailey, who trailed the Phantom around the mill and participated in his arrest, married his landlady, Daisy Dean, a year or two after receiving the reward money from the arrest. He remained with the Wheeling Steel mill police, and they resided in Bloomingdale. Clarence died at the age of sixty-two in 1948.

Arthur Lloyd Hooper, the Jefferson County prosecutor, won his election bid for common pleas court judge in 1936, less than two years after he successfully prosecuted the notorious Phantom murder case of Steubenville. Before that, he had served as Jefferson County's prosecutor from 1932 to 1936, when he took the bench. Hooper served in World War I in Company K, 332nd Infantry, as a first lieutenant. He even received a Purple Heart after being wounded in Italy. He served as a common pleas court judge for thirty-four years, until his death in 1970, at the age of seventy-eight.

Above: Arthur Lloyd Hooper's gravestone. *Opposite, top*: Ray Bliss Long's gravestone. *Opposite, bottom*: Ross Cunningham's gravestone. *From the collection of Susan Guy.*

Sheriff Ray Bliss Long led an unbelievably dedicated life of public service. He served in World War I, in the Twenty-Third Infantry, Second Division and saw the Battle at the Meuse-Argonne, one of the bloodiest skirmishes of the war (as did the Phantom, David Dasco). Ray served as a deputy sheriff under Sheriff William Yost from 1931 to 1933 and as a deputy sheriff under George Huscroft Sr. from 1960 to 1965. He also served as a township trustee for Cross Creek Township. He was the Republican nominee for sheriff in 1940, 1944, 1948 and 1952. He was superintendent of the highway department from 1954 to 1958. He was appointed street commissioner of Wintersville a few days before his death in 1965. He also served as president of the Jefferson County Agricultural Society. Ray B. Long met his death after a heart attack in 1965; he was driving northbound on State Route 43 in Wintersville, Ohio, when he suffered a heart attack, and his car went off the right side of the road and ended up in the yard of the former Alloway TV Repair Shop after hitting some mailboxes and a utility pole. He was seventy-five years old at the time of his death.

Steubenville police chief Ross Herold Cunningham was born on the site of the city building. He joined the Steubenville Police Department on April 3, 1922. On August 18, 1926, he was appointed acting chief of police by Mayor Edward Sander. The position became permanent on November 15, 1926, after Blaine Carter was ousted. Cunningham was a former president of the Ohio Association of Chiefs of Police. He served for thirty-nine years with the Steubenville Police Department. He died on January 8, 1967, at the age of seventy-six in Steubenville.

Harold Edwin "Babe" Morken, the twenty-nine-year-old millworker who was the first to identify the mill killer as David Dasco and report it on March 3, 1934, collected the largest rewards from both Wheeling Steel and the Jefferson County commissioners. He moved to Beaver County, Pennsylvania, shortly after the murders. He married in 1937 and died in Pennsylvania in 1986.

Thomas Joseph Dignan began his police career in 1910, when he was sworn in by Mayor Thomas Porter. He became the first detective in the Steubenville Police Department in 1914. Though he and his partner, Ernie Schroeder, were not instrumental in the capture of the Phantom, their tireless questioning of suspects and tracking down the gun's origin were crucial to the conclusion of the case. Dignan died on August 3, 1955, and was buried at Mount Calvary Cemetery in Steubenville. He was seventy-five years old at the time of his death. Ernest Henry Schroeder, the other half of "the Twins," teamed up with Tom Dignan to become Steubenville's super sleuths. He died on January 12, 1954, and was buried at Union Cemetery in Steubenville. He was seventy-four years old at the time of his death.

Thomas Rock, the lead defense attorney for David Dasco, was born in Rayland, Jefferson County, Ohio, on December 1, 1897. He practiced law in Steubenville during the 1920s and 1930s. He resided with his wife, the former Arilla Huff, at 216 South Third Street. Four years after the infamous

Thomas J. Dignan's gravestone. *From the collection of Susan Guy.*

Ernest H. Schroeder's gravestone. *From the collection of Susan Guy.*

Phantom Killer trial, Thomas Rock contracted pulmonary tuberculosis. He spent the last two months of his life at the Tuscarawas Sanatorium in Goshen Township, Tuscarawas County, Ohio. He died on April 9, 1938, at forty years of age. He was buried at Mount Calvary Cemetery in Steubenville, Ohio. Peter A. Gavin, a defense attorney for David Dasco, was born in Hammondsville, Jefferson County, Ohio, on November 27, 1873. He and his wife, Nancy, resided at 510 Dock Street. Gavin died at the Massillon State Hospital on September 4, 1949, at seventy-two years of age. He was buried at Mount Calvary Cemetery in Steubenville, Ohio. Simon F. Carpino, the third defense attorney for David Dasco, was born in Italy. He died at the age of eighty-seven in Jefferson County, Ohio. He was buried in Upland Heights Cemetery in Yorkville, Ohio.

24

THE SHERIFFS OF JEFFERSON COUNTY, OHIO

There have been forty-six sheriffs of Jefferson County, Ohio, since the town's formation on July 29, 1797. The following is a list of those sheriffs.

FRANCIS (FRANK) DOUGLAS
(around 1769–1830)

Francis Douglas served as the first sheriff of Jefferson County, Ohio, from 1797 to 1804. He resided in what is now East Springfield, Jefferson County, Ohio.

JOHN MCKNIGHT
(around 1772–around 1840)

John McKnight was the second sheriff to serve in Jefferson County, from 1804 to 1806.

JOHN GILLIS
(around 1780–around 1850)

John Gillis, the third sheriff of Jefferson County, served from 1806 to 1808. He was also a surveyor and a schoolteacher. As a surveyor, Gillis laid out the town of East Springfield, Ohio, in 1803; it was known as Gillis Town back then.

WILLIAM PHILLIPS
(1780–1852)

William Phillips served as the fourth sheriff of Jefferson County, from 1808 to 1812.

ROBERT CARREL
(around 1786–1826)

Robert Carrel served as the fifth and the seventh sheriff of Jefferson County, first from 1812 to 1814, then again from 1821 to 1824. He married Judith Noffsinger on August 9, 1819, in Jefferson County, Ohio. He died around 1826.

THOMAS ORR
(1770–March 29, 1828)

Tom Orr served as the sixth sheriff of Jefferson County, from 1814 to 1821. Thomas was a Scotch-Irish immigrant and came to the United States in 1790. He married Catherine Johnston while they were still in Ireland, and they had twelve children. Orr was an officer in the War of 1812. He died on March 29, 1828, in Steubenville and was buried at Union Cemetery in Steubenville, Ohio.

ROBERT CARREL
(around 1786–1826)

Robert Carrel was the fifth and seventh sheriff of Jefferson County, Ohio.

HENRY SWEARINGEN
(February 24, 1810–February 15, 1866)

Henry Swearingen, the eighth and tenth sheriff of Jefferson County, served from 1824 to 1828. He lived out his life in Brooke County, West Virginia. He died after falling down a flight of stairs and striking his head on the floor at the bottom. He was sixty-nine years old.

ROBERT THOMPSON
(1809–September 4, 1896)

Robert Thompson was the ninth sheriff of the county and served from 1828 to 1830. The lifelong resident never married. According to his obituary, he served again as a deputy sheriff under Moses Dillon in 1847, at the time of the Irish fights during the construction of the Pan Handle Railroad. He died of old age at his residence, just west of Union Cemetery, on September 4, 1896.

HENRY SWEARINGEN
(February 24, 1810–February 15, 1866)

Henry Swearingen was the eighth and tenth sheriff of Jefferson County, Ohio.

THOMAS CARREL
(around 1800–unknown)

Thomas Carrel was the eleventh sheriff and served from 1832 to 1836.

ISAAC W. MACDONALD
(1795–December 14, 1872)

Isaac MacDonald served as the twelfth sheriff of Jefferson County, from 1836 to 1839. He later moved to St. Louis, Missouri, where he died in 1872.

SAMUEL DIXON HUNTER
(1805–1852)

Sam Hunter was the thirteenth sheriff of Jefferson County, from 1839 to 1843. He was married to Mary Ann Buell and died in 1852, in Jefferson County, Ohio.

JAMES M. THOMAS
(December 29, 1810–June 19, 1888)

James M. Thomas was the fourteenth sheriff of Jefferson County, from 1843 to 1847. He married Sarah Margaret Carrel in 1837, in Jefferson County, Ohio. He was buried in Union Cemetery.

MOSES DILLON
(October 26, 1817–March 1, 1878)

Sheriff Moses Dillon. *Courtesy of the Steubenville Herald Star.*

Moses Dillon was the fifteenth sheriff of Jefferson County, from 1847 to 1855. During his time in office, the railroad was built in Steubenville. Irish workers were brought in to lay the tracks; they were from two rival counties in Ireland, causing a feud and numerous crimes, including housebreakings and murders. The jail—called the dark dungeon back then—was always full. This conflict between the Irish lasted through six sheriffs' reigns in office. After Dillon's terms as sheriff, he became a saloonkeeper. Sheriff Dillon was a friend of Edwin M. Stanton, Lincoln's secretary of war, during the Civil War. On May 9, 1863, Stanton asked Dillon to come to Washington, D.C., with him. Dillon made the mistake of telling Stanton that he had voted for Clement Vallandigham for the position of governor of Ohio. Vallandigham was the leader of the Copperhead faction of antiwar Democrats, and he was a former member of the Ohio House of Representatives from Columbiana County, from 1845 to 1847. Vallandigham, who was also a friend of Stanton, had been arrested in 1863, tried in a military court and exiled to the Confederacy. The indignant Stanton had Dillon, his former friend and sheriff, locked up until the war was over. Dillon moved to Illinois after his release. He died on March 1, 1878, in Illinois.

JAMES H. BLINN
(1808–September 24, 1885)

James H. Blinn, the sixteenth sheriff of Jefferson County, served from 1855 to 1859. He went on to serve as a general in the Civil War. One of the major cases of Blinn's term as sheriff came on August 14, 1859. Blinn, along with Mayor Oliver and U.S. Deputy Marshal Cable, raided the American House, where they arrested Robert Warrex for making counterfeit quarters. They confiscated the moulds, arresting Warrex and John Sutcliffe, the manager of the American House. Counterfeiting was a popular crime in the 1850s and 1860s, so to put a stop to it was a huge feather in the Jefferson County sheriff's cap. Blinn retired and was succeeded by John Moore. He died on September 24, 1885, and was buried at Union Cemetery.

JOHN MOORE
(June 6, 1822–December 25, 1898)

John Moore was the seventeenth Jefferson County sheriff, from 1859 to 1863. Prior to his election as sheriff, John farmed on his land, between Smithfield and New Alexandria. He became a steamboat captain on the river and followed that calling until he became sheriff. He married Mary Welday in 1843 and died on December 25, 1898.

GEORGE MCCULLOUGH
(December 8, 1805–August 25, 1889)

George McCullough was the eighteenth sheriff and served from 1863 to 1865. Born and raised in Cross Creek Township, near the fork of Wintersville Road, he was a well-respected man and a farmer. Soon after his failure to win the next election, McCullough and his family moved to Howard County, Missouri. He owned 373 merino sheep and made a living from shearing their wool. He died in Missouri on August 25, 1889.

AMBROSE UPDEGRAFF MOORE
(November 27, 1831–March 3, 1922)

Ambrose Moore served as the nineteenth sheriff of Jefferson County, from 1866 to 1870. He died on March 3, 1922, at his home at 1329 Euclid Avenue, Steubenville, at the age of ninety-one. After funeral services were held at his residence, he was buried in Smithfield. Moore was a first lieutenant in the Civil War, and his right elbow was shattered during the second day of the Battle of the Wilderness. He grew up with thirteen siblings in a log cabin that was built by his father in Smithfield Township. Moore was a farmer and noted auctioneer in Jefferson County.

THOMAS HUDSON MONTGOMERY
(1843–August 13, 1905)

Thomas "T.H." Montgomery, the twentieth in the line of sheriffs of Jefferson County, served from 1869 to 1873. Montgomery was born in Richmond,

Ohio. He died at his home in Toronto, Ohio, on August 13, 1905, and he was buried at Toronto Union Cemetery. He fought in the Fifty-Second Ohio Infantry during the Civil War. He married Kitty McClelland in 1876. His biggest problems in office were the number of escapes that happened, though it was widely known that the county jail was in very poor condition.

SAMUEL JOHNSON
(February 16, 1827–January 25, 1908)

Samuel Johnson served as the twenty-first sheriff, from 1873 to 1877. Born in 1827, in Tuscarawas County, Ohio, Johnson was orphaned when he was just a child. He ended up in Smithfield, Ohio, working on the farm of Joseph Cope, a prominent Quaker. Johnson and Cope aided escaping slaves on the Underground Railroad. He served in the 157th Ohio Infantry during the Civil War. Before becoming sheriff, he served as a deputy sheriff under both John Moore and Ambrose Moore. From 1879 to 1883, Johnson was superintendent of the Ohio Penitentiary Yards. From 1884 to 1888, he was an undertaker in Steubenville. Afterward, he returned to the Ohio Penitentiary and served as the superintendent of the penitentiary shops from 1889 to 1897. Johnson died on January 25, 1908, at the age of eighty-two and was buried in Smithfield, Ohio.

ALEXANDER SMITH
(August 19, 1830–August 19, 1897)

Alexander Smith, the twenty-second sheriff of Jefferson County, Ohio, was the son of Alexander Smith Sr., who laid out the town of New Alexandria, where the sheriff spent his childhood. Smith served as sheriff from 1878 to 1881. He was a captain in the 157th Ohio Valley Infantry and served first as a first lieutenant in the 52nd Infantry. He passed away of bronchial trouble on August 19, 1897, at sixty-seven years of age.

BENJAMIN MARTIN SHARP
(July 15, 1821–June 30, 1893)

Benjamin Sharp served the county as its twenty-third sheriff, from 1881 to 1885. He was a sergeant in the Fiftieth Regiment of the Ohio Infantry during the Civil War. The sheriff died on June 30, 1893, at the age of seventy-two. He is buried at Union Cemetery in Steubenville.

John G. Burns

(June 3, 1847–July 26, 1923)

John G. Burns served as Jefferson County's twenty-fourth sheriff, from 1886 to 1889. He moved to Chicago, Illinois, after his term as sheriff was over and became a successful real estate dealer. He later returned to Jefferson County and became a deputy sheriff. He died on July 26, 1923, and was buried at Union Cemetery in Steubenville.

Henry Opperman

(September 12, 1859–August 2, 1899)

Henry Opperman served as the twenty-fifth sheriff of Jefferson County, from 1889 to 1893. Known as "Honest Old Henry," Opperman also served on the Steubenville City Council, as the mayor of Steubenville and as the city street commissioner. While he was serving as street commissioner, he caught a cold that was followed by a heart attack and stomach trouble; this left him unable to leave his bed. He died at his residence at 507 North Fifth Street on August 2, 1899, at the age of seventy. He was buried at Union Cemetery in Steubenville.

Sheriff Henry Opperman. *Courtesy of the* Steubenville Herald Star.

John McCoy

(October 3, 1836–October 27, 1923)

John McCoy, the twenty-sixth sheriff of Jefferson County, Ohio, served from 1895 to 1897. He fought in the Civil War, with the Ninety-Eighth Regiment of the Ohio Valley Infantry. He was married to Mary Rickey Dinsmore. McCoy died on October 27, 1923, and is buried at Cross Creek Presbyterian Cemetery.

George Carrel Porter

(October 11, 1838–April 27, 1899)

George Carrel Porter, the twenty-seventh sheriff of Jefferson County, served from 1897 to 1899. He served in the Civil War and was wounded in Atlanta,

Georgia. He achieved the rank of captain. Before becoming sheriff, he was superintendent of the county infirmary for seven years. While on duty as sheriff, he ran along the train tracks near the Toronto Station, trying to catch the southbound train back to Steubenville. He was hit by the pilot bar of a train engine, fell and struck his head on the pilot bar. He died shortly thereafter. He had served sixteen months of his term in office. His son, Harry, who was also a deputy sheriff for his father, finished his father's term as sheriff. George Porter died on April 27, 1899. He was buried in Union Cemetery in Steubenville, Ohio.

Sheriff George C. Porter. *Courtesy of the* Steubenville Herald Star.

HARRY M. PORTER
(July 8, 1872–July 6, 1912)

Harry Porter was the twenty-eighth Jefferson County sheriff and served from 1899 to 1901. He stepped in to finish his father's term and was then elected for another full term. Harry died two days before his fortieth birthday in Scioto, Ross County, Ohio, where he had moved and was known as one of Ross County's leading citizens. He was out fishing with some friends on the day he died. He stepped into a hole that was thirteen feet deep and only a few feet in diameter and drowned. His body was recovered shortly after his death. His death occurred on July 6, 1912, and he was buried in Union Cemetery in Steubenville, Ohio.

RICHARD GILSON
(December 15, 1858–November 4, 1926)

Richard Gilson served as the twenty-ninth sheriff of Jefferson County, from 1901 to 1905. Before becoming sheriff, Gilson worked on the Cleveland and Pittsburgh Railroad, where he suffered the amputation of his right hand in an accident. He then became a telegraph operator in Rush Run, Rayland and Irondale. After that, he moved to Steubenville and served as sheriff for four years. Later in life, he was appointed postmaster. He died of blood poisoning brought on by a carbuncle at

Sheriff Richard Gilson. *Courtesy of the* Steubenville Herald Star.

his residence at 1302 Oregon Avenue. He lingered for eight weeks before finally dying on November 4, 1926; he was sixty-eight years old. He was buried at Union Cemetery in Steubenville, Ohio.

DUNLAVEY F. VORHEES
(June 6, 1852–May 5, 1920)

Dunlavey Vorhees was the thirtieth sheriff of Jefferson County, Ohio; he served from 1905 to 1908. In his early days, Vorhees attended Normal College in Hopedale, Ohio. He later went to Texas, where he ranched for five years. He then went back to Jefferson County, where he served as a deputy sheriff under John G. Burns. He remained with sheriffs Opperman, Porter and Gilson. Vorhees suffered a cerebral hemorrhage at the sheriff's office, and he died at his home three months later, when a blood clot formed in his foot and gangrene set in. He was sixty-seven years old at the time of his death, and he was buried at Union Cemetery in Steubenville.

JAMES MURRAY
(July 1, 1866–February 4, 1933)

James Murray was the thirty-first sheriff and served from 1908 to 1912. Murray, an Irish immigrant, came to America in 1883 and moved to Toronto, Jefferson County. He served as marshal of Toronto for nine years. He died of pneumonia at his home on Daniels Street on February 4, 1933; he was sixty-six years old.

WILLIAM ABRAHAM HUSCROFT
(July 16, 1868–February 11, 1951)

William Abraham Huscroft served as the thirty-second sheriff of Jefferson County, from 1912 to 1916. Huscroft was sheriff during many coal mine strikes; as many as sixty-five deputies responded with him to various incidents. In 1914, he foiled an assassination plot against him that he overheard being planned. Some men were going to break six prisoners out of the county jail; he prepared for the jailbreak with extra deputies and saved the day. Huscroft moved to Orange County, California, and died there in 1951. He was an uncle of future sheriff George Huscroft Sr.

JOHN LOWE MEANS
(July 25, 1870–June 30, 1918)

John Lowe Means was the thirty-third Jefferson County sheriff, and he served from 1916 to 1918. Means was born in his family's home on North Street in 1870. He worked in his family's foundry, was a county auditor and was the youngest man to serve in the Ohio House of Representatives—he was elected to two terms in the House. He was in the last half of his first year as sheriff when he died of a heart attack at the age of forty-eight. He was buried in Union Cemetery.

WESTERN TOLBERT BAKER
(November 29, 1860–June 3, 1950)

Western "W.T." Baker was the thirty-fourth sheriff of Jefferson County and served from 1918 to 1920. Baker stepped into the sheriff's office to finish the late John Lowe Means's term. Baker died on June 3, 1950, at eighty-nine years of age and was buried at Toronto Union Cemetery in Toronto, Ohio.

EDWARD DOLAN LUCAS
(April 7, 1873–December 7, 1953)

Ed Lucas was the thirty-fifth sheriff of Jefferson County, Ohio, and he served from 1920 to 1925. He worked as a deputy for Sheriff W.T. Baker. Lucas, the first sheriff to work during the Prohibition era, introduced the mugshot system in Jefferson County. He also had previous experience as a county detective. He died at the age of seventy-nine and was buried at Union Cemetery in Steubenville.

WILLIAM THOMPSON ALLISON
(October 28, 1883–July 13, 1963)

William Allison, the thirty-sixth Jefferson County sheriff, served from 1925 to 1929. Allison was a deputy sheriff under W.T. Baker and Ed Lucas. He was also the son-in-law of Sheriff W.T. Baker. Bertha Baker Allison, Allison's wife, died from a short illness at thirty-one years of age, leaving Allison with a young son, Robert. Both Allison and his son resided with his in-laws for a while until he remarried. He retired from Weirton Steel. William T. Allison died on July 13, 1963, at seventy-nine years of age, and he was buried at Union Cemetery.

WILLIAM JAMES YOST
(June 15, 1882–April 18, 1959)

William "Billy" Yost, the thirty-seventh sheriff of Jefferson County, served from 1930 to 1932. Yost was the third man to be elected to the office during Prohibition. He began his law enforcement career as a deputy sheriff under Sheriff Ed Lucas. After his term as sheriff was up, he became a deputy for Sheriff Robert "Dobbie" Bates and Sheriff Clarence "Whitey" Eberts. Yost was a plasterer and remained in that job for a long time. He died at his home at 1637 Oregon Avenue after a long illness. He was buried at Union Cemetery in Steubenville.

Sheriff William J. Yost. *From the collection of Susan Guy, photographer unknown.*

RAY BLISS LONG
(October 28, 1889–September 15, 1965)

Ray Bliss Long was the thirty-eighth sheriff of Jefferson County, Ohio, and he served from 1933 to 1937. He was a deputy sheriff under William Yost and George Huscroft Sr. Long served as a Cross Creek Township trustee, a trustee for Jefferson County Sportsman Club and a Jefferson County superintendent of the State Highway Department from 1954 to 1958. He was also in his third year on the Jefferson County Fair Board at the time of his death, which occurred on September 15, 1965. He suffered a heart attack while driving north on State Route 43 in Wintersville, Ohio. He ran off the roadway, into the yards of Earl Cramblett and Cecil Alloway, striking mailboxes and trees before coming to rest in the Alloways' yard. He was buried at Fort Steuben Burial Estates in Wintersville, Ohio.

ROBERT DOBBIE BATES
(January 22, 1901–January 5, 1955)

Robert Dobbie Bates, the thirty-ninth sheriff of Jefferson County, served from 1937 to 1948. Bates had a very successful record of arrests while in office, which caused a decline in crime. He instituted the fingerprint and photography department within the sheriff's office, and he started the practice of having a deputy lead funeral processions. He died at the young age of fifty-three in 1955. Bates was a professional baseball player and played with the Detroit Tigers before going to Jacksonville, Florida. He inherited his love of baseball from his stepfather, Johnny Bates, who was a major-league baseball player with the Boston Beaneaters in 1906. Johnny went on to play with the Chicago Cubs and Philadelphia Phillies, to name a few teams. Bates's grandfather John Watkins, whom he lived with as a child, built the first house on Pleasant Heights, at 1318 Park Street. Robert Dobbie Bates was buried at Union Cemetery in Steubenville.

CLARENCE ANDREW "WHITEY" EBERTS
(May 2, 1908–August 3, 1959)

Clarence "Whitey" Eberts was the fortieth sheriff of Jefferson County, Ohio. He served from 1948 to 1959, until his death. Eberts served as a deputy sheriff for three years under Sheriff Robert D. Bates. Eberts was a World War II veteran and married Phyllis Irene Tingey in her native England during the war. Phyllis was the first "war bride" of Jefferson County. The couple had a son, Patrick Robert Andrew Eberts, who died at the age of eleven, on February 22, 1959, from a perforated gastric ulcer. On August 3, 1959, at the age of fifty-one, Sheriff Eberts died of a liver ailment. His wife, a jail matron in his office, took over the reins as sheriff. He was buried at Mount Calvary Cemetery in Steubenville.

PHYLLIS IRENE TINGEY EBERTS
(June 20, 1915–June 29, 1966)

Irene Eberts served as the forty-first sheriff of Jefferson County, Ohio, after stepping in for her husband, Whitey Eberts, who died in office. She served from August 4, 1959, to 1961. She was the first and has been the only female sheriff to hold that office in Jefferson County. She had been a jail matron during her husband's administration. Born in England, she came to Jefferson County, Ohio, and earned the distinction as the first war bride of the county. She ran in a failed bid for sheriff in 1960. When George Huscroft Sr. became sheriff in January 1961, he retained Irene as an office deputy. Irene died in 1966 at the age of fifty-eight. She was found by a deputy on the floor of her bedroom, unconscious from a diabetic coma. An ambulance was summoned to her apartment at 309 North Third Street. She died three weeks later, on June 29, 1966, at Ohio Valley Hospital. She was buried with her husband and son at Mount Calvary Cemetery in Steubenville.

GEORGE LOUIS HUSCROFT SR.
(June 16, 1888–April 4, 1976)

George Huscroft served Jefferson County, Ohio, as its forty-second sheriff from 1961 to 1964. Huscroft was a World War I veteran and served with the 332nd Field Artillery Battalion in France at the Meuse-Argonne. He served as a deputy sheriff under Sheriff John Means and was twice elected as a Jefferson County commissioner. He operated a flower shop out of the former city annex building and a fruit and vegetable stand. Huscroft died at the age of eighty-seven in 1976, and he was buried in Union Cemetery in Steubenville, Ohio.

RICHARD PAUL WELLS
(September 9, 1929–April 13, 2001)

Richard Wells served as the forty-third sheriff of Jefferson County, from 1965 to 1972. He worked at Titanium Metals in Toronto and served as an Island Creek Township constable. After serving in the sheriff's office, he worked as a field representative for the Ohio Bureau of Motor Vehicles. He died in 2001 at the age of seventy-one and was buried at Union Cemetery in Steubenville, Ohio.

GEORGE LOUIS HUSCROFT JR.
(May 14, 1928–October 17, 2012)

George Huscroft Jr. served as the forty-fourth sheriff of Jefferson County, Ohio, from 1973 to 1978. George also served as a deputy under his father, George Sr. He retired from the Ohio Department of Transportation as an engineer. George died in 2012 and was buried in Union Cemetery in Steubenville.

GEORGE ANDREW THOMAS
(March 30, 1921–April 14, 1993)

George Thomas served as Jefferson County's forty-fifth sheriff, from 1979 to 1983. George served as a Steubenville police officer for twenty-four years. He helped form the Steubenville Police Community Service Bureau and was known as "Officer Friendly," giving talks to elementary schoolchildren. George served as a combat engineer in the Aleutian Islands from 1942 to

1945. He was a former president of Fraternal Order of Police Lodge 1. George passed away on April 14, 1993, at the age of seventy-three. He was buried at Fort Steuben Burial Estates in Wintersville, Ohio.

FREDERICK JOSEPH ABDALLA SR.

Fred J. Abdalla, the forty-sixth sheriff of Jefferson County, has been serving in that capacity since 1984. The beloved sheriff of the county formerly served as the mayor of Stratton, Ohio, for thirteen years. He also worked as a coroner's investigator for three years. Fred is a U.S. Army veteran; he served in Vietnam and earned many medals, including the Bronze Star. He is the longest-serving sheriff of Jefferson County, with thirty-five years in office.

BIBLIOGRAPHY

www.ancestry.com
Jefferson County Court Records
www.newspaperarchive.com
www.newspapers.com
Public Library of Steubenville
Steubenville Herald Star

ABOUT THE AUTHOR

S usan M. Guy was born and raised in Jefferson County, Ohio. The daughter of a police captain, Susan followed in his law enforcement footsteps. She was a police officer for fifteen years for the Cross Creek Township Police Department, achieving the rank of sergeant. She is currently a corrections officer for the State of Ohio, with over twenty-five years of service. She is a member of the Tri State Writers Society, a local writers' group, where she serves as the group's public relations director. Her debut book, *Mobsters, Madams & Murder in Steubenville, Ohio*, published by The History Press in 2014, was greatly received. *The Moonlight Mill Murders of Steubenville, Ohio* promises to be a thrilling follow-up.